DESPERATE FOR
NEW WINE

BOOKS BY DAVID HERZOG

Glory Invasion

Ancient Portals of Heaven

Mysteries of the Glory Unveiled

Living in the Glory Every Day

AVAILABLE FROM DESTINY IMAGE PUBLISHERS

DESPERATE FOR
NEW WINE

The Doorway into your Harvest

DAVID HERZOG

DESTINY IMAGE® PUBLISHERS, INC.

P.O. Box 310, Shippensburg, PA 17257-0310

*"Speaking to the Purposes of God for This
Generation and for the Generations to Come."*

Previously published as *Desperate for New Wine* by Xulon Press
Previous ISBN: 1-594674-01-9

This book and all other Destiny Image, Revival Press, MercyPlace, Fresh Bread, Destiny Image Fiction, and Treasure House books are available at Christian bookstores and distributors worldwide.

For a U.S. bookstore nearest you, call 1-800-722-6774.
For more information on foreign distributors, call 717-532-3040.
Reach us on the Internet: www.destinyimage.com.

Trade Paper ISBN 13: 978-0-7684-3221-3
Hardcover ISBN 13: 978-0-7684-3399-9
Large Print ISBN 13: 978-0-7684-3400-2
Ebook ISBN 13: 978-0-7684-9073-2

For Worldwide Distribution, Printed in the U.S.A.

1 2 3 4 5 6 7 8 9 10 11 / 13 12 11 10

Dedication

I want to dedicate this book to those who have been a source of blessing and inspiration in my life.

To Christ for the Nations Institute, which altered the course of my life during the time spent there. The spirit of prayer, evangelism, praise, worship, and missions that permeates the school was the launching pad for our ministry. Thank you, Mrs. Freda Lindsay, for keeping the flame burning.

To the faithful intercessors and supporters who have lifted their hearts to the Lord on our behalf during many crucial times. They are the ones who deserve recognition for all the souls who have been saved and healed and for every miracle that ever took place through our ministry.

Most of all to my family, starting with my precious wife, Stephanie Herzog. She has been a patient support during the many extra hours that this manuscript required, while we were on the mission field, going from meeting to meeting, and during the entire pregnancy and birth of our first child. Stephanie has been an inspiration to me as an incredible wife, mother, companion, minister, and friend as she has travelled the world with me spreading revival and winning the lost. The Bible says that every good gift comes from above (see James 1:17). When we first met in Bible school, I knew that she was God's gift to me.

To our first child, Tiffany Joy, who was filled with the new wine of the Holy Spirit while in the womb during the entire writing of this manuscript. When the original version of this book was finished, she was born. She is an overflow of the joy and love that the Lord has granted us during this renewal. May she be an arrow in the hands of our Lord even as a child. Also to Shannon Glory, who was born with the Glory of God all over her at birth, and to Destiny Shalom, who exudes the peace and favor of God, I love you all and am so proud of you!

Also to my mother, Colette, who has been an immense help in handling all of our administrative needs while we were overseas and who has been an encouragement to the accomplishment of this book. She has courageously smuggled Bibles into Cuba, traveled to China, and has boldly shared the gospel with her fellow workers without compromise. Thanks, Mom, for canceling your trip in search of Noah's Ark. Her example as a woman of prayer and her faithfulness to the Lord resulted in my salvation as a child. I'm forever grateful.

To my father, Victor, who has given in to the Lord after many years of trials. My deep love for him, and my earnest desire and compassion to see his salvation, birthed the evangelistic calling upon my life and the passion for the lost. You have come a long way, Dad! At the first writing of this book, he attended the same Bible school that I attended with my sister.

To my sister, Melissa, who once took a long and courageous missions trip to India and Bangladesh, during which she experienced floods, riots, having stones thrown at her, sickness—all of which she overcame—for the love she has shown to me as my only sister. I am thankful for the times she put up with me, her annoying older brother.

Acknowledgments

Special thanks to Francis Trees, pastor and missionary, for lending me his computer while he and I were both living overseas to write the first draft of this manuscript and especially for his friendship.

A *big* thank you to Sussan Esperanza, my mother-in-law, who flew across the Atlantic Ocean to help us care for our baby during the first month following her birth so that I could finish this book. She is a mighty woman of God and of prayer, a true servant of the Lord. We also thank William Esperanza, my father-in-law, for his love and timely support.

Special thanks to our good friend, Suzanne Ridner, for finding the time to edit this book.

I also want to thank Kevin Jonas for lending me his computer in the Christ For the Nations music studio during a ministry trip there.

Endorsement

The river of God is flowing in the form of a revival that is girding our globe. Some refer to it as *renewal,* meaning God is renewing something that has grown old. I prefer the term *revival,* which denotes new life. The world is not looking for a blessing (renewal) only; the world is looking for a change (revival). That longed-for revival is not coming; it is here. The natural progression from revival is an awakening.

One has to begin somewhere in this quest for God's choicest blessings. David Herzog has produced this volume to help direct a believer or a church in this quest. If you are hungry and willing to go after God, read on. This book is not meant for those who want a quick fix in developing a relationship with God that will bring revival. Total surrender is required. An open mind and heart are required. A holy life is required. An openness to the sometimes strange ways of God is required. A new love and new anointing are required. An acceptance of people is required.

I first met David Herzog in Paris, France, at a pastor's conference that I was conducting. It was immediately apparent that there is godly passion aflame in this young man's heart. This book is a product of that white hot heart *desperate for new wine*.

Carey Robertson
Assistant Pastor (during the Brownsville Revival)
Brownsville Assembly of God
Pensacola, Florida

Contents

Foreword

While David Herzog and his wife, Stephanie, were serving the Lord as missionaries to France, I enjoyed getting to know them. After times of ministry, we would have a meal in one of those quaint French restaurants. During those times of fellowship, breaking bread, I was able to gauge this young couple's zeal for the Lord's call to the nations and their intimacy with the Holy Spirit's presence, which I often refer to as "the glory." I discovered that David and Stephanie and even their young daughters were carriers of "the glory."

After a season of serving the Lord in Europe, God has moved the Herzog family to Arizona in the United States of America, though their mission continues to carry them to nations worldwide. As the years have passed, their zeal for "the glory" has kept increasing. I have personally seen this grace for unusual healings and miracles—accompanied with many turning their lives toward Christ.

From their home in France to their cottage in the foothills of Sedona, their journey with the Holy Spirit continues. This unique couple lives renewal and revival. And they always make the multitudes hungry for more of the reality of the miracle-working God.

Are you hungry for more of this wonder-working God? If you are *Desperate for New Wine,* David and Stephanie unlock wondrous new passageways into fresh intimacy with the Holy Spirit. I know that your fruit will be increased, as will the anointing and glory in your life.

In this hour, it is God's will to use every anointed believer in unprecedented ways to extend His kingdom so Christ may be glorified in all nations. This book is a special tool to assist you in this mission.

Dr. Mahesh Chavda

Introduction

After a time of intense hunger for more of the things of God, which steadily grew during the past few years, I began to sense that God was up to something. Yet I did not know what, where, when, or how. I had seen God do mighty signs and wonders and sinners repent at the salvation message during our meetings and on the streets, yet still there was something missing. These things were fine, but they were not quite revival. I knew that something was happening as the stirrings in my heart grew.

My wife and I began ministering in churches and meetings in the United States until God told us to leave everything and go to the nations. While in France, this hunger exploded. We decided to go on a tour of Israel for three weeks with Christ For the Nations Institute (CFNI) to see what God wanted to do with us there and to minister salvation to the people. This was a turning point. We were met by the living God in the Upper Room in a way that could only be described as new. After our experience in the Upper Room, we saw many conversions during our trip. More than that, we were changed.

Upon our return, I began to seek the Lord concerning our experience in the Upper Room. I began to hunger for more of what God was doing in this move, though I could not understand it all. This hunger led us to Toronto to receive more new wine. We thought we were there to visit some relatives, but God had other plans. We were filled with a new love for Him and a new anointing after our encounter in Israel. From there, renewal spread wherever we ministered throughout the United States and Europe. More than with just signs and wonders, God is now changing the hearts of His people and renewing them toward revival.

While ministering under this new anointing, we noticed that some churches and Christians lacked an understanding concerning how to receive renewal and God's purposes for renewal. Some who received the new wine did not know where to go from there or how to maintain it on an ongoing basis. On New Year's Eve, the Lord challenged me to write this book as a blessing to God's people. I believe He desires it to be a tool to spread this move of the Holy Spirit from renewal to revival—to help us focus our sights not only on renewal but on where it is going on a global scale. I decided to obey Him.

Much of the content and principles in this book were given to me by the Lord as revelation, especially during times of fasting and prayer. The other parts are based on our experiences with the new wine of His Spirit as we are seeing renewal and revival occur in different nations where we minister. This book was written to give you an understanding of the crucial times that we are in and to inspire you to seize this moment in history.

Those who desire renewal but are skeptical and want some answers, and those who may have had a taste of the new wine but don't want it to stop there, will find this book a valuable tool for increasing renewal in your personal walk with the Lord, your church, and your ministry. This book is truly for those who are *Desperate for New Wine!*

CHAPTER 1

Empty Your Waterpot

On the third day there was a wedding in Cana of Galilee, and the mother of Jesus was there. Now both Jesus and His disciples were invited to the wedding. And when they ran out of wine, the mother of Jesus said to Him, "They have no wine." Jesus said to her, "Woman, what does your concern have to do with Me? My hour has not yet come." His mother said to the servants, "Whatever He says to you, do it." Now there were set there six waterpots of stone, according to the manner of purification of the Jews, containing twenty or thirty gallons apiece. Jesus said to them, "Fill the waterpots with water." And they filled them up to the brim. And He said to them, "Draw some out now, and take it to the master of the feast." And they took it. When the master of the feast had tasted the water that was made wine, and did not know where it came from (but the servants who had drawn the water knew), the master

*of the feast called the bridegroom. And he said to him,
"Every man at the beginning sets out the good wine, and
when the guests have well drunk, then the inferior. You
have kept the good wine until now!" (John 2:1-10)*

As Jesus and His disciples were invited to the wedding at Cana, so Jesus is symbolically inviting us, the present-day Church, to a celebration of joy—a holy party in honor of our soon-coming King! Many Christians and leaders around the world are sensing that this is a historic time for the Church and that we are on the verge of a spiritual breakthrough worldwide.

The wedding party is ready and the invitations have been sent. Everything is looking good except the wine. There isn't enough! Someone must find some new wine. What a shame it would be for the bride if all the invited guests come in only to find that there is no more wine!

God's people are becoming hungry and thirsty for a fresh outpouring of the Holy Spirit. The past Charismatic movement is losing its fervor and in many aspects is becoming a tradition. Many mainline and Charismatic churches and denominations are attempting to give an invitation to the world to come, yet their numbers are dwindling. They are becoming desperate just to survive. The people come in apathetic, dissatisfied, and spiritually undernourished. What is the problem? The problem is that the wine is running out!

In many countries, and especially during the time of Jesus in Israel, wine was a must for a wedding. To run out of wine during a wedding would have been a major catastrophe that would not be so easily forgotten. It would have been the talk all over town. Many churches are embarrassed because they are inviting in the people, but have no wine to give. Yes, their sermons are doctrinally correct, yet there is something missing. What is missing is the fresh out-pouring of the Holy Spirit that renews, refreshes, and restores.

Some would go so far as to even fake it. But anyone who is thirsty and comes to drink of the presence of the Holy Spirit will know the difference if he goes home still dry and thirsty. The world is tired of hype and frills.

What happens when the wine runs out? Christians pretend they still have it or they talk about the good old days. Eventually, a religious spirit takes over, and a once-blessed church becomes a boring, lifeless, structured system without a sense of expectancy from 10:00–12:00 Sunday morning. The service is all prearranged without the thought of what the Holy Spirit may want to do. This is what many call "church." No wonder the world is not running into our churches! Instead, they are seeking elsewhere to fill their thirsty souls with "New Age" philosophy, the occult, materialism, and other traps that lead to destruction. We are as responsible to our generation as King David was when he desired to *"serve his own generation"* (see Acts 13:36).

OUT OF WINE

And when they ran out of wine, the mother of Jesus said to Him, "They have no wine" (John 2:3).

Many people are doing different things to attempt to fill their churches and personal lives with what is missing. People run to one seminar after another, only to return empty. Churches in the same dilemma often struggle to find the latest church growth programs that will work in keeping their people motivated.

Mary, the mother of Jesus, was wise. She knew exactly what to do to solve this problem. She went directly to Jesus. This is so simple, yet we often miss it. We need to go to the Master, the source of

23

all things. Mary is the example we need to follow in this regard. When there is a problem or lack in our lives, we need to seek the face of God first.

Personally, when Stephanie and I began to seek God for the deeper and more intimate relationship with Him that we so hungered for, at that time He began to change our personal walk with Him and our ministry. This led us to receive this fresh move of the Spirit that is presently being poured out in many nations.

I believe the primary key in receiving this blessing is to be desperately hungry and thirsty for more of God—and not just that, but for a total transformation of our lives, as Peter had at Pentecost. Before Pentecost he had the anointing, to a degree. He was powerfully used, yet he still failed the Lord, fled when his life was at stake, and denied that he even knew Jesus. After Pentecost, Peter was a changed man, full of such boldness that he preached to the very people he feared only ten days earlier, commanding them to repent of their sins and reminding them that it was they who delivered the Messiah to be crucified.

What led to such a transformation? I believe that after Peter had denied Jesus, he began to evaluate his life and ministry. He realized that he did not have all that it takes to fulfill the Great Commission. How could he obey the Lord's command and yet be lacking so much? He also realized that there were some things in his life that needed to go. He most likely shed many tears in the Upper Room as God was emptying out and cleaning this vessel in order to fill it with something more powerful—new wine.

We are the Peter generation! We need to come to the end of ourselves, realizing that we can't fake it any longer. We need a total emptying, cleansing, and purification in order to be refilled and revived and enter into this new, fresh worldwide move of the Spirit.

Mary was honest about the situation at the wedding party. There wasn't enough wine to make the party a success. She was willing to face the facts and deal with them by humbling herself and asking Jesus for help.

If we become honest before God at our insufficiency and allow our hearts to be broken, then God has something to work with. God gives grace to the humble, but resists the proud (see James 4:6; 1 Pet. 5:5). The way of brokenness before the Lord is the way to the new wine. Yet with each death to self on the cross, there is a resurrection.

EMPTYING THE WATERPOTS

Now there were set there six waterpots of stone, according to the manner of purification of the Jews, containing twenty or thirty gallons apiece. Jesus said to them, "Fill the waterpots with water." And they filled them up to the brim (John 2:6-7).

Jesus asked the servers at the wedding to do a strange thing! Why would anyone pour water into dirty waterpots instead of the wineskins? These waterpots were used for the purification of the Jews! That means that they were dirty and most probably full of dirty water used by the religious Jews to clean themselves. I'm sure that the servants of the wedding feast emptied out the dirty water and cleaned the vases as any good servant would do before filling them up with drinking water and serving it. If you would grab a glass full of dirty water, how would you fill it up with fresh water unless you emptied and cleaned it out first?

Jesus was symbolizing something very important. Before we can receive a fresh filling of the Holy Spirit, we ourselves must first be emptied out and cleaned up. Our vessels have become dirty because many of us have become stagnant in our anointing and walk with God.

Old wine that has become stale is like a stream that stops flowing and becomes a stagnant pond; no new water is flowing in and no old water is flowing out. When this happens, we become religious and in great need of a total cleansing and purification. Maybe at one time there was a fresh anointing, a close communication, and a strong presence of God on your personal life and ministry. But if there has been no release, then the scent becomes like a nice smelling perfume mixed with perspiration. There must be an emptying process before receiving. How can it be released?

Often as we minister in different places—no matter what country we're in—when we pray for people to receive this new wine of the Holy Spirit, the person we're praying for will often weep uncontrollably like he or she never has before. Whether the person is a pastor, leader, or church member, the same occurrence often takes place. At times it is very dramatic and quite shocking for some who are not used to seeing such brokenness and weeping, especially if it is accompanied with loud cries. Many have not really been able to cry in years. People are often getting rid of past hurts, bitterness, sin, religiousness, etc. These wounds often go as far back as their early childhood. Whatever it is, it must be emptied out before receiving the joy of this new wine which can often be accompanied with laughter.

All of this is part of the healing and restoring process of the Church and is done under the anointing of the Holy Spirit. For some, it is triggered by a simple word of prophecy or encouragement that God is healing them of rejection in the past. Still others need repentance under the conviction of the Holy Spirit.

There seems to be a spiritual principle here that is repeated throughout the Scriptures: the principle of giving and receiving. It is much more than a financial principle of blessing. Before we receive something new from God, He demands that we let go of some things.

Sin can also be the problem that hinders a person from receiving this spiritual blessing. If this is the case, there is only one solution for emptying dirty water.

Then Peter said to them, "Repent...and you shall receive the gift of the Holy Spirit" (Acts 2:38).

True repentance is a sure way of allowing God to cleanse and purify us in preparation for a fresh filling of the Holy Spirit. The same goes for receiving the baptism of the Holy Spirit for the first time. It is only possible after repenting of sin and accepting salvation.

IN THE UPPER ROOM

I began to receive the new wine of the Holy Spirit on an evangelistic outreach to Israel with my wife in May 1994. During the three weeks we saw quite a number of Jews and Palestinians find salvation. We were with an outreach team from Christ For the Nations Institute totaling 76 people.

One day we were in the Upper Room in Jerusalem worshiping the Lord. This was a time when my wife and I really began to develop an intense hunger and longing for a fresh touch of the Holy Spirit upon our lives. As we began to worship, an unusually powerful yet gentle presence of the Holy Spirit filled the room. It began to increase very rapidly. During this time, I noticed a dove flying back and forth above our heads in the room. It was another sign to me that the Holy Spirit was at work. Suddenly, several people fell down onto the floor after being prayed for (Charismatics call this being "slain in the Spirit").

Unexpectedly, a Jewish man with a beard rushed up to the front of the group to receive prayer. He was not part of our group. The team began to pray for him. His wife began weeping and pleaded with me to pray for him. She told me that they were actually fellow believers like us and had been ministering in Israel for many years. God was now directing them to be sent out as missionaries. She explained that the Holy Spirit told them that morning to go immediately to the Upper Room to receive a special anointing for their ministry. As I approached her husband, he opened his eyes and said, "Prophesy to me, son, you have a message for me."

I responded, "Well, hold on. Let me ask the Lord first if He has a prophetic word for you. I'm not going to fabricate something!" Immediately God gave me a specific word for him. As I spoke the word, the Holy Spirit commanded me to blow on him, which was not a habit of mine. I obeyed and I blew on him, similar to what Jesus did to His disciples.

And when He had said this, He breathed on them, and said to them, "Receive the Holy Spirit" (John 20:22).

Instantly the man fell down as if being slammed to the floor, shaking under the power of God. He had received much more than a prophetic word. It was something extraordinary from God.

Shortly after this incident, I went to the back of the crowd and began to lift my hands and praise God for what had just happened. Then I began to cry like I've never cried before. For one thing, I was so humbled to actually relive Acts 2 in the Upper Room in Jerusalem where it all happened on the day of Pentecost. As I was weeping, something very strange took place. My legs started shaking and vibrating almost uncontrollably. Then I found myself on the ground, having fallen down sometime during all of this by His power. I wept all the more, not fully understanding exactly what was happening to me and why I was crying so much.

All I knew was that it felt like a total cleansing and a freedom from the burdens and anxiety of ministry. The concerns of life were totally in the Lord's hands. A transformation had taken place that I had never known before. I had rarely been "slain in the spirit" in past years, though I had prayed for many who were. Then, as I opened my eyes, I saw a team member prophesying to me about our ministry and the new things God had in store for us. The prophecy was right on and confirmed what God had already been speaking to us. Eventually I slowly attempted to get back on my feet. I remained stunned even hours later, crying all over again without really knowing why. It was a mystery at the time, yet it felt so good. God's presence was ever so strong. I had my first of several encounters with the Holy Spirit that day that would forever mark my life and ministry under this new anointing.

What happened in that room was more than what happens when many receive the baptism of the Holy Spirit and speak with other tongues but then let it stop there. I was being emptied, refilled, and prepared for a new and fresh outpouring of the Holy Spirit. I began to be filled with the new wine of the Holy Spirit.

TEARS

Those who sow in tears shall reap in joy. He who continually goes forth weeping, bearing seed for sowing, shall doubtless come again with rejoicing, bringing his sheaves with him (Psalm 126:5-6).

If those invited to the wedding party are still holding on to their heavy loads, they will not be able to enter into the joy that the new wine brings. They may come expecting to be filled with joy, but there is a process to go through.

More often than not, those who will let go of all barriers and not resist the gentle, yet powerful touch of the Holy Spirit will end up sowing much in tears. Much of it is releasing dirty water like bitterness, discouragement, anxiety, past hurts, sorrow, and suffering that have never been fully dealt with. Being emptied of all of these things allows the next phase of this renewal to take place in a person's life. This applies to both leaders and church members.

Of course, this is not a set of rules, but it is generally what is taking place in this new move around the world. Some people have had more suffering and hurts than others, and they may spend more time in this phase of weeping. Others cry less, or sometimes not at all, yet seem to immediately receive the joy and even laughter prevalent in this renewal. This is also another reaction which we will cover in the next chapter. Whatever the reason for tears, if the Holy Spirit is activating them, crying is a good thing that should not be neglected.

> *Return and tell Hezekiah the leader of My people, "Thus says the Lord, the God of David your father: 'I have heard your prayer, I have seen your tears; surely I will heal you. On the third day you shall go up to the house of the Lord'"* (2 Kings 20:5).

Many have been crying out to God for years to release them from certain trials and suffering. Finally, as the Holy Spirit breaks through internal blockages, there is a release and even tears of joy.

> *But Esau ran to meet him, and embraced him, and fell on his neck and kissed him, **and they wept*** (Genesis 33:4).

The guests invited to the wedding party have to deal with the other guests whom they may not have gotten along with in the past. Drinking this new wine together provides an atmosphere that makes it easier to forgive and reconcile. The party is the only time many of the guests will have the opportunity to face their adversaries and declare peace.

Jacob and Esau were brothers who had become enemies, yet God was reconciling them and working on their hearts. Don't forget that Jacob also wrestled with God just prior to this for the blessing he was determined to receive. We too will have to wrestle with certain issues if we want His blessings upon our lives. In this fresh outpouring, some people weep because God is healing His children of wounds, rejection, and division that have been among brothers and sisters, parents and children, and ministers for too long. As these things are dealt with, tears will flow.

TEARS AND BROKENNESS

*"Now, therefore," says the Lord, "Turn to Me with all your heart, with fasting, with **weeping**, and with **mourning**." So rend your heart, and not your garments; return to the Lord your God, for He is gracious and merciful, slow to anger, and of great kindness; and He relents from doing harm. Who knows if He will turn and relent, and leave a blessing behind Him—a grain offering and a drink offering for the Lord your God?* (Joel 2:12-14)

A blessing especially comes when the tears become tears of true repentance. When tears like this flow out of a recognition of sin and disobedience, there is a great reward, as we will see later on in the chapter of Joel about the promise of a mighty worldwide outpouring of the Spirit. Tears are instrumental to unlocking the door to our hearts and igniting personal revival. I'm not suggesting trying to dig up past sins and fabricating tears. The Holy Spirit's presence in this move will convict our hearts and we will go with the flow of what He wants to do in our lives, allowing ourselves to be broken—unless we resist Him.

31

Most great revivals started this way. The Azusa Street Revival was a revival of tears at the beginning, which lasted over three years and spread revival all across the globe. Often proud and arrogant men came to the Azusa meetings to "make their mark" only to be found on the floor in repentance. A preacher came from Chicago to expose the meetings as a fraud. When he walked into the mission, a 13-year-old girl approached him, and said, "Thus saith the Lord, 'You have come to expose these people. Yet, I have brought you here for another purpose...'" After the man's heart was exposed he fell to his knees in repentance, broken by Lord in His mercy.

Frank Bartleman (1871-1936), a Holiness evangelist, wrote, "The preachers died the hardest, they had so much to die to: so much reputation and good works." He also wrote, "I would rather live six months at that time than 50 years of ordinary life."[1]

William Seymour, a very humble, black Baptist pastor who had lost one eye from smallpox, sparked the Azusa revival. Because of segregation laws, he had listened outside the doorway to hear William Parham (1873-1929) teaching about the Holy Spirit. As he did, his hunger intensified for the baptism of the Holy Spirit in his own life.

William Seymour moved to Los Angeles to seek God's face for this experience in the Holy Spirit. He was invited to preach in a church in Los Angeles with the possibility of becoming the pastor. He was quickly locked out of the church after he preached on the baptism of the Holy Spirit. He himself had not yet received this baptism before preaching about it. God allowed Seymour to go through these experiences of brokenness, which he did not resist. As his hunger grew, the trying circumstances allowed him to depend all the more on God's grace.

This brokenness and hunger soon exploded into the greatest modern-day outpouring of the Spirit in early 1906. Meetings were first held on the front porch of a private home. When they grew too large, they were finally held at 312 Azusa Street, which had once been an African Methodist Episcopal church, and then later a livery stable and a warehouse for a department store. Racial barriers were broken, and there was no trace of racism in the meetings at a time in history when tension between different races was at a height.

The whites came with love and true repentance for the way they felt about blacks and how they had treated them. The blacks came with love and true forgiveness. Other races participated similarly. It was a revival of brokenness. Arthur Osterberg, who loved the whole revival ever since its conception, said:

> The Azusa Revival began where every revival should rightly begin, in repentant tears. It began in tears, it lived in tears and when the tears ended, the Azusa Revival ended.[2]

The results of this revival, sparked by a true hunger for the fullness of the Holy Spirit, were phenomenal. According to Vinson Synan, a church historian, by 1980 more than 50 million people had been affected by the Pentecostal movement. A *Christianity Today* Gallup Poll showed 19 percent of all adults (29 million persons 18 and older in the U.S. alone) identified with this renewal in 1980. It became the foundation for the Charismatic-Pentecostal outpouring. By 1990, more than 372 million people had been affected by this one outpouring of the Spirit at Azusa, which ignited simply because a person such as Seymour allowed God to break him in humility and thus release God's Spirit. For that we should be forever thankful.

I thank God that the apostles and the rest of the believers in the Upper Room stayed there and persisted with the Lord, allowing their hearts to be broken until the blessing came. Imagine what results the present renewal could bring the world in the coming days! If you are full of old wine that has turned into bitter vinegar, allow the Holy Spirit to empty it out to make way for the new wine of the Spirit. Don't fear the tears and the brokenness. If God exposes your heart to you and it breaks you, continue to let God have His way with you. He will empty you until there is room for unspeakable joy to flood your soul.

Those who sow in tears shall reap in joy (Psalm 126:5).

ENDNOTE

1. Frank Bartleman, *The Azusa Street Revival,* (Revival School, www.revivalschool.com). The entire book can be read at http://associate.com/groups/anzac/www/Azusa-Street++.htm.

2. Nelson: Ph.D. Thesis (Birmingham, 1981), 66-67 n. 10.

CHAPTER 2

Unspeakable Joy

*A merry heart does good, like medicine, But a broken
spirit dries the bones* (Proverbs 17:22).

And wine that makes glad the heart of man...
(Psalm 104:15).

Now that the waterpots have been emptied and
cleansed, they are ready to be filled. Some of the older
guests remark, "This is not like the old wine that we
are used to drinking."

*So they were all amazed and perplexed, saying to one another,
"Whatever could this mean?" Others mocking said, "They are
full of new wine." But Peter, standing up with the eleven, raised
his voice and said to them, "Men of Judea and all who dwell in
Jerusalem, let this be known to you, and heed my words. For*

these are not drunk, as you suppose, since it is only the third hour of the day"(Acts 2:12-15).

The ones mocking may very well have been the religious crowd. Anyhow, these people knew very well how to spot a drunkard, having accused them of such. What does a drunk person normally do? He talks, but often we can't understand what he is saying. He will often fall to the ground. He may cry. He tends to say things very boldly that under normal circumstances a sober person may never dare to say. He will laugh when intoxicated.

All of these are likely to happen in this new move of the Spirit. People falling under the power of God has become more and more common in the last several years. What is new to many is the supernatural joy often manifested by laughter, bringing with it a new boldness to speak the message that God has for this generation.

At the outset of this new outpouring of the Holy Spirit, many branded it as a "laughing revival." Laughing is actually only one of many manifestations that occur in renewal, due to unspeakable joy. It is biblical and very much needed in the Body of Christ today. The renewal of new wine is as much a time for joy and laughter as it is a time of weeping and releasing our stagnant, dirty water.

One thing is certain according to God's Word: we must judge these manifestations by their fruit. What is the fruit? For many people who laugh like this, the joy is a source of deep healing. Many Christians have not laughed in years. Church, in the world's eyes, is often known for being sad, boring, lifeless, and without joy.

God is changing that. He is restoring joy back to His Church, the joy of knowing that God truly loves His people. This joy is a real phenomenon because often it is seemingly uncontrollable, yet it is under God's control. That seems to be the problem for some. If they can't control it, they don't want it! The Holy Spirit is asking the

Church to please let go of the control over ourselves, others, and churches, and let Him take control.

As far as the question, "Why do people laugh?" I would like to use one evangelist's simple yet clear explanation, "People laugh at my meetings because they are happy."

FILL THE WATERPOTS

Jesus said to them, "Fill the waterpots with water." And they filled them up to the brim (John 2:7).

The servants dash off in search of new wine at Jesus' command. The guests are coming in by the droves. The master of the feast is getting slightly worried wondering if the servants will bring in enough wine to satisfy the guests and those who are still to arrive. Jesus reassures him that the servants will come with waterpots of wine that have been filled!

We mentioned the process of being emptied out in the previous chapter and what part tears play. After this phase, we feel very light but empty. Now we are much more prepared to be filled with the new wine without breaking our wineskin because it has become new.

Notice that after the servants brought the waterpots, Jesus wanted the pots to be filled to the brim. Some people will take just a little and go. Then they wonder why it faded out. Jesus is asking you and me to come thirsty for a full infilling of His Spirit. When you are full to the brim, you will easily overflow and spill. This is where the laughing often comes in. The more we come, the more we are filled with the new wine of the Holy Spirit. When someone is very full of this new joy, it is very contagious and can spread with ease.

That is why at our meetings we encourage people to be prayed for several times until they have fully received. Many people are so used to going up for prayer and then immediately going back to their seat. To go back a second time for prayer would seem to be a lack of faith to some people. This is a tradition that must change! Often the minister who practices this may also feel embarrassed that the job didn't get done the first time he or she prayed. To those in this category, don't worry. Even Jesus prayed twice until the blind man was totally healed—not halfway healed (see Mark 8:22-25). Our motivation should be to see the other person fully blessed until he or she has received to full capacity. If the people are still hungry and thirsty for more of God, by all means don't stop them! It is actually a sign of ever-increasing faith, not a lack of it.

Blessed are those who hunger and thirst for righteousness, for they shall be filled (Matthew 5:6).

Another reason to seek prayer several times is that some people may be prayed for once and then get emptied out and need more prayer to be filled. We must become true servants, like those at the wedding in Cana, when serving this new wine. The servants filled the waterpots in order to serve all the guests. We must receive as much as we can of this anointing—not just for ourselves but enough to satisfy others as well.

REJOICE

Be glad then, you children of Zion, and rejoice in the Lord your God; for He has given you the former rain faithfully, and He will cause the rain to come down for you—the former rain, and the latter rain in the first month. The threshing floors shall be full of wheat, and the vats shall overflow with new wine and oil. So I will restore to you the years that the swarming locust has eaten, the crawling locust, the consuming locust, and the chewing locust, My great army which I sent among you (Joel 2:23-25).

Applause and sighs of joy illuminate the wedding party. What is all the commotion about? The servants have arrived with waterpots that have been cleaned and are almost bursting with new wine. Just when they thought the party was dying out, it turns out to be only the beginning! It is a time of rejoicing! Why? Because the new wine has arrived as the old wine has run dry.

What is there to rejoice about? The Holy Spirit is putting this joy into the hearts of His people for one great reason. He is pouring out His Spirit over all the earth as He promised He would in the last days. In this passage from Joel, we are commanded to rejoice at God's faithfulness in past times when He gave us the rain of His Spirit. Ever since the day of Pentecost, He has been pouring out His Spirit on different generations. We often rejoice over past revivals and moves. But it does not stop there. God will restore everything that we ever hoped for in our generation concerning revival.

That is still not the end of it. He said that He would restore whatever He gave in the past, and give us the latter rain as well. This is what seems to be happening right now. He is restoring the fullness of the Holy Spirit. Many of these manifestations, as we will cover later, are recognizable in history books written on past revivals. As well as this joy, other characteristics such as a greater boldness to witness, an increase in the prophetic, inner healing, and deliverance from bondages, are taking place.

This joy will allow such a change in people's lives, they will never be the same again. It's exciting to see this joy transform people who were depressed, hopeless, and suicidal. We have also seen ministers and pastors who were on the verge of giving up receive this joy. Instead of bitter and stagnant ponds, which often kill the fish and all the life forms they come in contact with, their lives, marriages, and churches are becoming fountains of living water.

A joyful church is a victorious church! It attracts the unsaved to at least check out the party. Now that the rain is falling, we need to ask the Father to keep the rain pouring in increasing measure. Once you have tasted the new wine of the Holy Spirit, one drink will not be enough. You will want more! Ask for more rain in the time of the latter rain!

> *Ask the Lord for rain in the time of the latter rain. The Lord will make flashing clouds; He will give them showers of rain, grass in the field for everyone* (Zechariah 10:1).

Don't be satisfied with only a few drops of new wine. Keep asking for more!

PERSONAL EXPERIENCES

My first experience at a renewal service took place in July 1994 in a church in Canada, where much of this renewal had gained worldwide attention at the time. We were only in that area to visit some of my wife's relatives and preach in a Methodist church—or so we thought. On my way there, I crossed paths with pastors and Christians in churches where we ministered who urged and encouraged me to check out the renewal service.

As we walked into our first renewal meeting, it appeared to be pretty normal for a Charismatic church in July. The people were casually dressed. They sang some great songs and the presence of God electrified the place. Then it got interesting. As the speaker just talked or shared some Scripture, for no apparent reason, half of the congregation laughed hysterically. The speaker just continued speaking until he was finished. The laughing exploded at times when the speaker tried to be the most serious. The odd thing was that there was nothing funny in what he said. Evidently, there was either a wonderful joy in the place or there was a joke that I didn't catch. It was no joke—this was the result of the Holy Spirit at work. Other manifestations took Stephanie and me by surprise, such as shaking and trembling. Some of these other manifestations I'll cover in a later chapter.

Naturally speaking, it seemed like a very bizarre meeting. Part of my problem was that I did not understand what was going on in the Spirit at the time. As I closed my eyes to pray for direction, the Holy Spirit gave me a peace and commanded me first not to judge or criticize what I did not understand. Second, He instructed me to receive from Him this blessing that I had sought and had begun to receive when I was in Israel in the Upper Room.

While we were there, we noticed many people going up for prayer and coming back changed. We recognized an actress and also evangelist Reinhard Bonnke's lead intercessor, both of whom were receiving mightily from the Lord. We also saw pastors and leaders who came from practically every denomination in existence. And so Stephanie and I went up for prayer and fell out under the power of God. This happened each time we went for prayer. I did not really feel anything at all except the Holy Spirit pushing me to the ground. Apart from that, I did not laugh, scream, or shake. One thing was certain: we believed by faith that something new was imparted to us, which later became evident.

The next day, I preached in a Methodist church. The Lord told me to preach on the baptism in the Holy Spirit without omitting anything like tongues, signs and wonders, etc. I was a little hesitant, knowing that this was not a popular subject, but decided to be wise and obey the Lord. What made things worse was that they had a second speaker who used to be a Catholic priest before becoming a Methodist preacher. He happened to also be the apostle who started that very church and several others in the area. He graciously told me to feel free to share whatever I had, and that he would confirm and add to whatever I shared. Now I knew for certain that I was in for trouble! The Lord has a sense of humor.

So I shared with the church about the Holy Spirit without compromising anything on the subject. Stephanie and her family had a slightly tense look on their faces, not knowing what to expect. Then the second speaker took the platform. He began to also preach about the Holy Spirit, attempting to confirm my sermon. At first, he preached quite cautiously, but eventually confirmed that what I had shared was definitely in the Word of God. At the end, I did an altar call and the people came forward.

Then God began to move. One girl began to laugh and shake. Others received healing. A woman's sight was fully recovered. Another man felt an intense heat on his back, like a fire, resulting in physical healing. Some began to cry, not knowing why. Afterward, many started to ask questions. They did not know that these things still could happen today. It was a joy to see that the people were touched and changed by this fresh anointing. It was then that I realized I had caught something at the renewal meetings—whether I liked it or not.

Something new was happening in our ministry. We were used to seeing people fall, receive healing from sicknesses and diseases, and even receive great miracles. But the difference was that these other manifestations also began taking place at our meetings very frequently and with no warning.

Several days later we ministered in the town of Sedona, Arizona— my hometown. I shared about Philip the evangelist in the Book of Acts. It was not a funny message at all, but as I was speaking, practically everyone began to laugh uncontrollably. I was appalled, but I proceeded with my sermon nonetheless. The more I kept speaking, the more they laughed, until I could hardly continue anymore. People were falling from their chairs laughing so hard that their stomachs began to hurt, including the pastor, his wife, and my own wife.

I wasn't sure if they were laughing at me or not, so I stopped and asked why they were laughing. Did I miss another joke? They didn't know how to explain it to me. I figured that no one had paid attention to what I preached since they were all caught up in laughter. Afterward, the pastor and several others told me something very interesting. They said that they were listening to every word I said even though it appeared otherwise. They even recited my sermon back to me. They also remarked on how the message had really blessed them.

The rest of that week became more and more intense with physical healings, signs, and wonders. The Holy Spirit was doing things His way for a change, and He did not ask us for our permission. Whether or not we understand everything about this joy is not the issue. We must allow Him to fill us and our churches with such a joy that it changes our lives.

I've noticed that when the spirit of joy is prevalent, the anointing is also much stronger to perform miracles, and everyone's faith seems to soar. Barriers of doubt, negativity, and other hindrances are dispelled much more quickly.

The joy of the Lord needs to saturate us and our churches. For too long we have been satisfied with dull and depressing church services, meditating on our sins instead of the fact that we can be set free from sin through repentance. This seems to be the accepted form of church life for many Christians. With this often being the case, would it be such a problem if people are so full of joy that they can't help but laugh?

God is inviting His Church to celebrate His presence and His soon return. Many weep every time they see a cross. Jesus is asking us to also rejoice that He has been resurrected! Many cathedrals are marked by a crucifix, leaving an impression of defeat and mourning. This is how millions of people see Jesus today—they don't realize the fact that He is actually alive, seated at the right hand of the Father, having overcome death itself. When we look upon the cross, we should not only see the incredible suffering He went through, which certainly should never be forgotten, but we need to rejoice that He paid this price so we would not have to die in our sins. If He did not pay this price, then there would be a legitimate reason to begin mourning, as we would be without hope.

Recently a pastor friend and I walked the streets of Paris, France, with a big wooden cross. We tried to be serious about it as we interceded for the city. Soon though, we were laughing, full of the joy of the Lord. We passed by a bar as the people stared with a curious amazement. The joy of the Lord mocks at the superficial joy that the world gives. That is why Jesus went all the way to the cross, for the joy set before Him.

JOY IN TRIALS

Therefore we also, since we are surrounded by so great a cloud of witnesses, let us lay aside every weight, and the sin which so easily ensnares us, and let us run with endurance the race that is set before us, looking unto Jesus, the author and finisher of our faith, who for the joy that was set before Him endured the cross, despising the shame, and has sat down at the right hand of the throne of God (Hebrews 12:1-2).

This joy that Jesus had before Him even gave Him the ability to endure the cross. We will always have trials and tribulations. In fact, the more of the Holy Spirit we receive and the more we are used, the more we will encounter trials. But this joy seems to carry us through. This is the joy that allows Christians in persecuted countries of the world to endure hardship. The early Church was sorely persecuted yet persecution did not stop them. They grew bolder! At Pentecost they began to receive the new wine that filled them with indescribable joy. This joy was for healing and comfort but it was also for a much greater purpose. It was to be the force that kept them evangelizing the world fearlessly. The accusation that they were drunk in the Book of Acts was partly true. Peter did not deny this fact.

Peter declared to the mockers in Acts 2:15, *"For these are not drunk, as you suppose."* These Christians were drunk with the heavenly wine, not in the manner that they were thinking. In Ephesians 5:18 we are commanded not to be drunk with wine. Instead it instructs us to be *"filled"* with the Spirit. Drunkenness is being filled to capacity. Not just partly filled. We are to be filled to capacity with the heavenly wine. Drunkenness with earthly wine is a sin. Drunkenness with heavenly wine is a command. People in this lost world often drink in order to numb the pain in this life, only to find it again the following day.

When we are filled with the new wine it will allow us to look beyond persecution, pain, fear, intimidation, and any other obstacle that would come against us. The wine must overflow to such a degree that we can be a bold witness in the days ahead, no matter what persecution might come our way. This was the secret of the early Christians and those at present in persecuted countries. When we pray for revival we cannot afford to bypass the renewal.

Without renewal, revival can be dangerous. We must enter this first phase of revival, which is preparation. Without renewal we will not be able to contain the increase in spiritual power that accompanies revival. Our wineskins will burst under the pressure. God wants to strengthen and repair our wineskins first!

Stephen, the first Christian martyr, knew this joy. It was the same joy that Jesus knew that enabled Him to suffer the cross. Surely Jesus was *filled* with the same joy that took Him through the painful cross He chose to bear.

> *But he, **being full of the Holy Spirit,** gazed into heaven and saw the glory of God, and Jesus standing at the right hand of God, and said, "Look! I see the heavens opened and the Son of Man standing at the right hand of God!" ...And they stoned Stephen as he was calling on God and saying... "Lord, do not charge them with this sin." And when he had said this, he fell asleep* (Acts 7:55-56;59-60).

Most Western Christians are not filled with this overcoming joy. I don't mean the superficial smile at church when the pastor asks us to greet someone. Many Christians in our society are even afraid of what their co-workers would think of them if they knew that they went to church. And this is in a free country where Christians are not being thrown into prisons or experiencing persecution because of their faith. Somehow, speaking in tongues and shouting "Praise the Lord!" is not enough. We can and must attain the fullness of the Holy Spirit if we don't want to be limited to simply an outward sign or the salvation experience alone.

Paul and Silas also knew this joy amidst a dark and dirty prison:

> *Then the multitude rose up together against them; and the magistrates tore off their clothes and commanded them to be beaten with rods. And when they had laid many stripes on them, they threw them into prison, commanding the jailor to keep them securely. Having received such a charge, he put them into the inner prison and fastened their feet in the stocks. But at midnight*

Paul and Silas were praying and singing hymns to God, and the prisoners were listening to them (Acts 16:22-25).

What a witness they were to the prisoners who had lost all hope! Even the guard and his family received salvation because of this explosive joy. Only a supernatural joy could have caused Paul and Silas to endure such circumstances with a song in their heart that ultimately led to the opening of the prison doors. Even Peter, the night before he was to be executed, slept so soundly in his prison that the angel sent by God had to shake him in order to wake him up (see Acts 12:1-7). This joy that he knew overcame his fears and brought him peace in a most terrifying situation.

This joy with the manifestation of laughter has reportedly been prevalent during past decades in countries such as Argentina, China, and Russia. It was a forerunner that led to revival even amidst great persecution. This powerful joy is no joke; it is a must that you and I in the Western world desperately need. It has the ability to take us through the process of renewal to revival in these endtimes, as the Bible and history itself clearly point out.

When the persecution increased in the early Church the believers knew that within themselves they needed more of God in order to make it through the tough times. They went back to God and asked for boldness. What they received was another refill of the new wine. They were once again filled with the Holy Spirit and received the same joy and boldness. Once you have been filled with new wine and it begins to run dry, ask God for another serving! He is a generous God.

"Now, Lord, look on their threats, and grant to Your servants that with all boldness they may speak your word, by stretching out Your hand to heal, and that signs and wonders may be done through the name of Your holy Servant Jesus." And when they

had prayed, the place where they were assembled together was shaken; and they were all filled with the Holy Spirit, and they spoke the word of God with boldness (Acts 4:29-31).

Notice carefully in this passage that the joy that the early Church received was to be ultimately directed toward a specific purpose. The purpose is to preach the gospel, heal the sick, cast out demons, and become a powerful witness to the saving power of God.

ABRAHAM'S JOY

At the wedding at Cana, some impatient guests get a bit tired of waiting for the new wine. They ask Jesus, Mary, and the master of the feast if the new wine will really arrive as they entertain thoughts of leaving the party. Those who have faith that the new wine will arrive will stay and not be sorry they did.

> *"And I will bless her and also give you a son by her; then I will bless her, and she shall be a mother of nations; kings of peoples shall be from her." Then Abraham fell on his face and laughed, and said in his heart, "Shall a child be born to a man who is one hundred years old? And shall Sarah, who is ninety years old, bear a child?"* (Genesis 17:16-17)

Abraham laughed at the promise, yet it was not a sarcastic doubting laugh. He actually believed God, and a joy filled him up to such an extent that he laughed at the impossibility of man and the greatness of God in the situation. Many are in a desperate situation in their lives and ministries. It looks like there's no way out, and no way to be blessed and bear fruit. In the natural, it is true. In the past few years I've met more burned out and frustrated pastors and leaders who are on the verge of spiritual devastation and hopelessness than ever before. Most of them have great promises from God about their lives and ministries that never seem to be fulfilled.

Now that the Holy Spirit is pouring out this new wine of joy, it is healing the past hurts, restoring faith and confidence in God's promises, and changing churches and nations toward revival. Joy is more powerful than we think. We need more of it to survive the storms of this life.

Therefore Sarah laughed within herself, saying, "After I have grown old, shall I have pleasure, my lord being old also?"...But Sarah denied it, saying, "I did not laugh," for she was afraid. And He said, "No, but you did laugh!" (Genesis 18:12,15)

Too many people are like Sarah. Her laugh may have been one of doubt, mockery, and stubborn unbelief. It seems that it goes one of two ways. Many people are getting a revelation of this joy as Abraham did. And likewise, there are others who criticize the laughter, rebuking those who are experiencing it and judging what God is doing. This is a very quick and effective method for quenching the Holy Spirit in their own lives.

Others mocking said, "They are full of new wine" (Acts 2:13).

Just because we may not understand what is happening, it's not a license to begin judging and attacking what God may be doing in a person's life.

Those who receive this joy are also acquiring strength to be overcomers, and they are seeing their promises fulfilled as Abraham did. Others are mocking and becoming like Sarah, only to produce an Ishmael with more strife and division (see Gen. 16: 21). Let us ask God for joy that brings faith to believe in His promises and that will mock the enemy's lies of impossibility and hopelessness.

Consider it pure joy, my brothers, whenever you face trials of many kinds (James 1:2 NIV).

…Weeping may endure for a night, but joy cometh in the morning (Psalm 30:5 KJV).

A LOOK AT HISTORY

During the revival in the 1700s in the United States, Jonathan Edwards (1703-1764) in his manuscript entitled *A Narrative of Surprising Conversions* wrote:

> It was very wonderful to see how persons' affections were sometimes moved when God did, as it were, suddenly open their eyes, and let into their minds a sense of the greatness of his grace, the fullness of Christ, and his readiness to save—after having been broken with apprehension of divine wrath, and sunk into an abyss, under a sense of guilt which they were ready to think was beyond the mercy of God. Their *joyful* surprise has caused them, as it were, to leap, so that they have been ready to *break forth into laughter,* tears often at the same time issuing like a flood, and intermingling a loud weeping.[1]

Laughter and tears were commonplace in this revival that shook the country. Charles Finney (1792-1875), after receiving the baptism of the Holy Spirit, wept so loudly and profusely that a church choir member knocked on his door, only to find him in total surrender before the Lord. She asked him if he was sick or in pain. When Finney was able to speak, he said, "No, but so happy that I cannot live."[2]

The Welsh revival was marked by joy. This is what one visiting journalist wrote while watching Evan Roberts lead the meeting.

The dominant note of the revival is prayer and praise. Another striking fact is the *joyousness and radiant happiness* of the evangelist. It has been remarked that the very essence of his campaign is mirth. To the rank and file of ministers, this is his most incomprehensible phase. They have always regarded religion as something iron-bound, severe, even terrible. Evan Roberts *smiles when he prays, laughs when he preaches.*[3]

Evan Roberts, who was the primary instrument God used to ignite and guide the Welsh revival, was especially noted for his unusual joy. George T.B. Davis' report to America after visiting the revival stated:

I have just returned from a two-day visit to the storm center of the great Welsh revival which is sweeping over Wales like a cyclone, lifting people into an ecstasy of spiritual fervor…A hymn was now started, and my attention was riveted on Evan Roberts, who stood in the pulpit and led the music with *face irradiated with joy, smiles, and even laughter.* What impressed me most was his utter naturalness, his entire absence of solemnity. He seemed just bubbling over with sheer happiness, just as jubilant as a young man at a baseball game. He did not preach; he simply talked between the prayers and songs and testimonies and then rarely more than just a few sentences at a time.[4]

Jonathan Edwards began to trace the link between great joy and times of tears and brokenness in this account:

The unparalleled joy that many of them speak of is what they find when they are lowest in the dust, *emptied most of themselves,* and as it were annihilating themselves before God; when they are nothing and God is all; seeing their own unworthiness, depending not at all on themselves, but alone on Christ, and ascribing all glory to God. Then their souls are most in the enjoyment of satisfying rest; excepting that, at such times, they apprehend themselves to be not sufficiently self-abased; for then above all times do they long to be lower. Some speak much of the exquisite sweetness, and rest of soul, that is to be found in the exercise of resignation to God, and humble submission to his will. Many express earnest longings of soul to praise God; but at the same time complain that they cannot praise him as they would, and they want to have others help them in praising him. They want to have everyone praise God, and are ready to call upon everything to praise him. They express a longing desire to live to God's glory, and to do something to his honor.[5]

...In Your presence is fullness of joy; at Your right hand are pleasures forevermore (Psalm 16:11).

The guests and the bride will never be the same after the joy of the new wine hits them. Though outwardly it may not be altogether understandable, it is evident that the new wine is not like the old. It brings even greater joy to the soul and is the life of the party. What is a wedding party for anyway? It is a time of rejoicing and laughter, enjoying constant refills of the new wine!

ENDNOTES

1. Jonathan Edwards, *A Narrative of Surprising Conversions,* ed. Jay P. Green Sr., (Lightning Source, Inc., ISBN 1-5-58960-021-5), 26.

2. Charles Finney, *Memoirs* (New York: A.S. Barnes & Co., 1876), 20, 21.

3. George T.B. Davis, *When the Fire Fell, The Million Testaments Campaigns* (1945), 23. Emphasis added.

4. Ibid., 27.

5. Edwards, 47.

CHAPTER 3

Receiving New Wine

Jesus said to them, "Fill the waterpots with water."
And they filled them up to the brim (John 2:7).

God is willing to give this new wine to anyone who will receive it. There are several conditions to receiving, which I would like to address to those who have never received or have trouble receiving. It can be frustrating at times to see other people blessed by this renewal while you stand there wondering why you are not able to receive anything. You may be imagining what in the world could be wrong with you. Some people may even be tempted to entertain animosity toward God and the whole move.

As we mentioned in Chapter 1, often people will need a total cleansing and emptying that only the Holy Spirit can work out before being filled. From our frequent prayers for people to receive the new wine, we have realized that for many hungry Christians just one minor tip makes all the difference in the world to receiving. Knowing the conditions and protocol for receiving new wine can save time and avoid confusion.

HUNGER AND DESIRE

Blessed are those who hunger and thirst for righteousness, For they shall be filled (Matthew 5:6).

Now that the new wine has arrived, some of the guests are having a communication problem. They don't all seem to get served. What they don't realize is that this is a very expensive wine. The servants are not about to serve this wine unless they are absolutely certain that the guests truly desire it. As a guest you must give clear signals to the servants that you are really thirsty if you want to be served. More often than not you have to humble yourself and get up out of your chair to make your desire for new wine very clear!

One of the most important keys to receiving is being hungry for a move of God in your life. Those who receive the most are those who are desperate and starving for more of God in their lives. That is why people will travel halfway around the world to certain places to receive new wine. Those who do this often leave their families and ministries and spend their savings just to receive. To some it is foolishness. Yet one thing is for sure, the people who do this normally come back full because of their hunger and determination to receive.

Many who live day in and day out in such a renewal often complain and wonder why they are not always receiving as much as others who come from far away. It's a question of how desperate you are to receive. Those who travel far and wide in search of renewal will check into a hotel and find much more time to seek the Lord before the meetings, being away from the busyness of work and ministry.

Whatever condition it takes to get alone with God to be full of personal revival is worth it.

When the gold rush hit California, people traveled far and wide across the continent in hope of finding gold in order to strike it rich. Likewise, when there is a shortage of water in many developing countries, people will travel for hours and even days by foot to get the water. They know it's their only source of survival. They are desperate and thirsty.

The Church today is in the same desperate need of the new wine of the Holy Spirit. The old wine is running out! Go wherever you can to find the river where the fresh waters of the Holy Spirit are flowing. Stay until you are full of renewal and bring it back to your church, city, and nation. This is not a fad. It's a matter of spiritual survival for the days that lie ahead. You can't justly criticize a person dying of thirst if he or she travels far and wide to find a source of water.

It is true that one does not necessarily have to go far to find this refreshment. Yet some people are so desperate that if they know of a spring, though it may be far, they won't waste any time but will just go. It's much easier to go where you know it is bursting with renewal, and it is easier to receive as there is a much higher level of expectancy.

If you seek the Lord with all your heart you will be filled. He will show you what to do and where to go. It may be during a time of fasting and prayer that you receive. Most people, though, receive this outpouring by either going somewhere where it is happening or by a ministry coming to their church and "serving" the new wine. As mentioned, my wife and I began to receive this blessing on an evangelistic outreach to Israel, and then afterward God led us to receive more in some powerful renewal meetings. Eventually, God showed us how to receive the new wine directly from Him. We learned to maintain the new wine and drink in more whenever we became dry, instead of always importing this anointing. We'll talk about this aspect of maintaining the new wine in the next chapter.

The important thing is to be hungry and thirsty for more of Him, and then you can be constantly filled. If you don't have the hunger and desperateness that you should, then don't feel condemned—just ask Him to put it in you. He may empty you out of all your securities that keep you satisfied with your spiritual life as it is until you are broken before the Lord. Whatever it takes, it is worth the price because you will have more to give once you are emptied and filled.

RECEIVE BY FAITH

Some wedding guests are not quite sure that they will receive new wine even if they signal the servants. They half-heartedly raise their hands and the signal is not clear. You, as a guest, must have faith that if you ask for this wine you will receive it. Don't play games with yourself. Ask, knowing that you will receive!

The most elementary condition for receiving anything from God has always been the same. We receive by our simple childlike faith. By faith we believed in Jesus and were saved. By faith we receive healing. By faith we receive the baptism of the Holy Spirit and anything else from the Lord. Some people have the idea that they have to feel something each time or see some kind of vision or be visited by angels before believing that they have received. Others believe that they have not yet received anything because they are not experiencing a certain manifestation that they have observed with someone else.

When I first received this new anointing, I received it by faith, trusting God that something had been imparted to me. In the beginning I felt nothing in particular, nor did I receive an incredible revelation at the time. I simply believed that I had received something new from God. Only several days later did we see this new wine flood the churches we ministered in with different things occurring in our meetings that were new to us. Then we saw the evidence of our childlike faith, though we still did not fully understand it all.

When we had first asked to receive this blessing we could have thought to ourselves, *Oh well, I guess it was not for me.* If we had left thinking that, because we saw no physical evidence, we would have left empty. It is often true that the people who receive the most don't always have the immediate outward manifestation as it is evidenced later on. We cannot judge by outward manifestations alone.

You must go before God with the attitude that you will receive for no other reason than the fact that the Bible says that whatever you ask in prayer by faith you will receive, as it is in accordance with the will of God. It is definitely God's will for you to be renewed with a new joy and anointing that will transform your life and others around you.

> *So I say to you, ask, and it will be given to you; seek, and you will find; knock, and it will be opened to you. For everyone who asks receives, and he who seeks finds, and to him who knocks it will be opened. If a son asks for bread from any father among you, will he give him a stone? Or if he asks for a fish, will he give him a serpent instead of a fish? Or if he asks for an egg, will he offer him a scorpion? If you then, being evil, know how to give good gifts to your children, how much more will your heavenly Father give the Holy Spirit to those who ask Him!* (Luke 11:9-13)

Fear is one of the biggest opponents to your faith and will often hinder you from receiving anything from God. Some people are afraid of this new move of God mostly because of manifestations. They are afraid that they might receive a demon instead of the Holy Spirit. This should not be our fear if we trust our heavenly Father. The Word of God tells us that if we ask our Father for bread, He won't give us a stone. He certainly will not give you a demon if you ask Him for more of the Holy Spirit and His presence in your life!

Another fear that people sometimes experience is the fear of falling. Some have had a bad experience in the past when someone supposedly under the anointing pushed them hard enough to make them fall to the floor. The person doing this perhaps wanted to make himself appear very anointed, though he manipulated the situation. Don't let these past experiences hinder you from receiving. Just focus on Jesus, and if you find yourself on the floor, that's fine. If you are still standing, that's still fine. Falling—or any other phenomenon—is not necessarily a sure sign of receiving, though often it points to His powerful force at work.

What I've noticed when the new wine of the Holy Spirit is in abundance is that often the anointing can get so strong that people begin to fall to the floor before any hands are ever laid on them. Often people just cannot stand as the glory of God is too strong to handle standing up. Our natural bodies can only absorb so much of the Spirit before they begin to manifest by falling, shaking, laughing, etc. Don't get distracted by manifestations or try to receive a certain manifestation. Just receive more of Jesus and ask for His love with full assurance.

Often while ministering I will ask people to receive directly from the Holy Spirit before waiting for us to personally pray with them. The result has been that scores of people in the meeting will suddenly fall like dominoes onto the floor by the power of God. One man asked a pastor if he could lie on the floor before receiving prayer so that way the whole issue and his fear of falling would not distract him from receiving. He did just that and was able to receive much that night. Just simply ask for the bread of Heaven instead of worrying about what will happen when you receive.

> *But without faith it is impossible to please Him, for he who comes to God must believe that He is, and that He is a rewarder of those who diligently seek Him* (Hebrews 11:6).

We must have a faith that believes in a good and giving Father, a faith that is persistent and diligent in seeking Him. We receive the reward of our faith when we come with the attitude that no matter what it takes, we are going to receive all of Him that we can. With this motivation our reward is not far away. A closer and more intimate communion with God our Father is well worth it.

It appears that those who are young or new converts find receiving much easier than others. The reason is that they often already have a childlike faith that simply just receives. We need to return to that childlike faith! It is not an impossible task if we are older or have known the Lord for many years; it is mainly a simple attitude problem. Become like a child.

Losing Control

When the invited guests come, they sit down and they are served new wine. Some get to this point, lift the cup to their lips, take a sip to refresh themselves, and then stop right there, going no further lest they also be carried away by the potency of the new wine. They have a fear of not being able to contain themselves. These are guests who want to stay in control.

Imagine that you have been searching for days for drinking water in a desert under the scorching hot sun in 100 degree weather.

Then finally you find a flowing river. Automatically you will want to take a drink and wet your feet. You want to cool off some more, so you decide to go in waist deep. Holding to a nearby boulder, you attempt to go even deeper into the charging water. You go neck deep to really get refreshed. At this point you are still holding onto that rock for your dear life, lest you be carried away by the river's strong current.

Many people are in this dilemma. They want to get their feet wet and are in great need of being cooled off and renewed. The only problem is that they don't go all the way in. Many people will begin to receive and taste of this fresh renewal. They may even pray, "More, Lord!" But when it gets to the point to where the water comes up to their heads, and the force of the current causes them to slowly lose their grip from the rock, they begin to back off and slowly get out of the river.

The problem is control. They began to realize that if they allow their lives and churches to flow into this river of the Holy Spirit, then they will have to let go and lose the control. They don't mind a little refreshing, but they don't want to lose the grip they have on their churches, ministries, or reputations. When you have one hand gripping onto a rock and your feet in the river touching the ground, even though you're partly in, you are still the one holding onto the control.

The Holy Spirit is challenging Christians and leaders to submerge themselves in the river, let go of the control that we hold over our lives and ministries, and be guided by the river of the Spirit. There comes a breaking point where we either go all the way or we settle for just a little. It's a matter of trusting God to take over our churches, lives, and ministries as we are swept into His current, thereby handing Him all the control. The Holy Spirit is challenging His people to go all the way with Him.

Either this renewal is of God and will usher in revival in our personal lives, churches, and cities, or it is not of God. If we truly believe that it is of God, then we need to allow the Holy Spirit to have total control. It's like when I drive my car. I never used to let anyone but myself drive my car with me in it. I would always insist on doing the driving as I simply felt more comfortable behind the wheel. To a certain degree, this was an indication of a fear of letting someone else take the wheel and handing over the control.

Individuals, churches, and ministries who are going all the way, allowing the Holy Spirit to take over, are seeing their lives and churches bearing much fruit with an ever-increasing anointing of God. This is part of the reason why churches and individuals will enjoy some of this new wine for several weeks, and then later wonder why it left. In the following chapter I will explain how to keep the new wine from slipping away like this.

The Holy Spirit is faithful. If He has the control, He will do a better job than we ever could, and He will give us clear directions instead of us giving Him directions. Don't be satisfied with just an experience. Let this move of God permeate your life and ministry until it develops into an explosive revival that will shake cities and nations. We need to capture this moment in history. This kind of an outpouring comes less than once in a lifetime! We are fortunate to be living in such a time as this!

DON'T ANALYZE

There are different types of guests at this party. Some would love to have deep intellectual discussions about the wine, analyze all the effects and the pros and cons, yet never actually taste it. All of this conversing and analyzing has little meaning because until they have tasted it, they will never really know what it is. They'll continue to stay trapped inside their own logic wanting to figure it all out first.

Perhaps you can relate. You stand there waiting to be prayed for. Someone comes and begins to pray with you. You wonder if you are actually going to receive, or if the person praying really has the anointing. Suddenly, you feel a warm presence. You question if what you are sensing is really of God or a figment of your imagination. Then you feel like you are about to fall, and the presence of the Holy Spirit gently (or forcefully) sways you toward the floor. Immediately you open your eyes to make sure that you have not been pushed or manipulated, only to realize you were not. As the anointing gets stronger upon you, you begin to take a step backward, and then another, and again another so as not to fall down. What you have just done is to analyze and refuse to give the control over to the Holy Spirit. This creates a major blockage to receiving. Your natural mind takes over, cutting off the Holy Spirit's control.

God wants to confound our natural minds. We don't need to understand it all and have everything mentally under our control before receiving. This can especially be a problem among Christian leaders, those in a position of authority, and intellectuals who are used to making a constant assessment of any given situation, as they are usually the ones responsible for whatever happens. This can be overcome by simply focusing our minds and thoughts on Jesus, and not on what we see, hear, feel, or don't feel. At times we will need to discipline our minds and tell them to rest and be at peace as we continue to keep our attention on receiving.

We need to once again receive as a child would to overcome these barriers. Our minds will tend to complicate things. A child-like faith is one that will confound the logic of our developed thinking process. We must come to the point where we want all of God, whether or not we understand all that may entail.

Did you understand everything about Jesus and salvation before accepting Him? No, but you knew that your life was empty and sinful, and that Jesus could change that and fill your void. Later you learned more about Him, and hopefully you have come to know Him better each day. If you had decided to wait until you understood every angle about Jesus and the Bible, you would never be saved to this day.

The same thing goes with receiving the baptism of the Holy Spirit. Did you understand how people spoke in tongues or prophesied when they received the baptism in the Holy Spirit? No, but you knew that the power of God was there and that you desperately needed that power to help you to be bold and victorious in your Christian life. Compared to the early Christians in the Bible, you knew your life was lacking. Later on you continued to learn about the Holy Spirit and how He operates, though we are all still learning about Him. It is no different when receiving the new wine of the Holy Spirit. There may be some new manifestations you don't quite understand, but the same principle and the same Holy Spirit are involved.

Imagine a boy caught in a tree. His father says, "Jump, son, I'll catch you!" The trusting little boy simply jumps without thinking twice as to whether or not his father will really catch him. Some of us are like the little boy caught in the tree, yet we respond to God's invitation by measuring the distance between ourselves and the ground and saying, "Wait, if I jump, how can I be sure You will catch me?" We may continue to reason, "Perhaps it's not even my Father telling me to jump into His arms!" It takes this kind of person much longer to let go of the security of the tree and receive help from the Father.

When you have total trust and confidence in your heavenly Father, there is no need to fear. This fear is the root cause of all the analyzing. You may have been taken advantage of by other so-called father figures. You must let His love overcome this distrust.

There is no fear in love; but perfect love casts out fear, because fear involves torment. But he who fears has not been made perfect in love (1 John 4:18).

NOT BY WORKS

The most offensive guests are those who try to pay the master of the feast to make sure that they get served. These are the most offensive, as they have a hard time receiving. The wine is free and can only be received in that manner. The servants are offended at the thought that anyone would try to pay off the master of the feast while others are getting the wine free. There are no exceptions—everyone must receive it by faith, free of charge. You cannot earn it. After all, each guest is there by invitation. It's not a restaurant; it is a wedding party. Anything else is considered a bribe.

Oftentimes people who have the hardest time receiving the new wine are those who think they can get their prayers answered by earning it. Quite often when I begin to pray over people to receive the new wine, the person will begin to violently pray in tongues until they are blue in the face, begging God to please fill them. Usually I will ask the person to simply stop praying, relax, and just receive.

To many it seems impossible not to do the work of praying in order to receive. When you received Jesus, it was by faith, not by your persistent begging prayers. If you were to offer a gift to someone, it would seem quite strange if the person responded by begging you to give it when you had just told them it was theirs to take. Once you decide to stop trying to impress God and just soak in His presence, you can receive much more easily.

This striving is also like two people on opposite sides of a one-way street, pushing the same car in the opposite direction to each other. The car doesn't move very far that way, unless someone gives up and allows the other to push. It's much easier to give up and let God work on our behalf.

You can't earn this blessing because it is received by faith. Not faith in your prayers, but faith in His grace. This kind of faith knows that if God doesn't fill you up, it won't happen by your works. This is having faith in His grace instead of faith in your faith.

For by grace you have been saved through faith, and that not of yourselves; it is the gift of God, not of works, lest anyone should boast (Ephesians 2:8-9).

This can be a very humbling passage when you understand exactly what Paul is really saying here. Even the faith we claim to have is not ours to begin with. It is given to us by God. So, if God doesn't give us faith, we cannot believe. Therefore, we cannot boast about even the faith we have because it is not ours to begin with. God gives each man a measure of faith.

At first, when I started to dig into this truth, I thought, *Well, what's the use of praying for anything if it is all by grace?* The fact is that the two work together. Some would say, "God will do what He wants when He wants." Others believe their faith alone will make God work on their behalf. Each of these truths taken to an extreme, without the balance of the other, will eventually go off on the wrong track. It's a balance of the two. When you accepted salvation, you were saved not by your works, but because of God's grace. On the other hand, the only way to obtain that grace is by your faith, actually reaching out and taking it saying, "I accept it." That is the only way to obtain it. Here the two, faith and grace, work side by side.

Our will must reach out and accept this present renewal by faith. This renewal is a free gift of God's grace. It's so simple that it can be complicated. The best way to understand it is to read the Scriptures as a child would and accept His gift as a child would.

Extra Oil

Then the kingdom of heaven shall be likened to ten virgins who took their lamps and went out to meet the bridegroom. Now five of them were wise, and five were foolish. Those who were foolish took their lamps and took no oil with them, but the wise took oil in their vessels with their lamps. But while the bridegroom was delayed, they all slumbered and slept. And at midnight a cry was heard: "Behold, the bridegroom is coming; go out to meet him!" Then all those virgins arose and trimmed their lamps. And the foolish said to the wise, "Give us some of your oil, for our lamps are going out." But the wise answered, saying, "No, lest there should not be enough for us and you; but go rather to those who sell, and buy for yourselves." And while they went to buy, the bridegroom came, and those who were ready went in with him to the wedding; and the door was shut. Afterward the other virgins came also, saying, "Lord, Lord, open to us!" But He answered and said, "Assuredly, I say to you, I do not know you." Watch therefore, for you know neither the day nor the hour in which the Son of Man is coming (Matthew 25:1-13).

We are in a season in the Body of Christ when the Holy Spirit is asking us not to be satisfied with the measure of oil in our lamps but to take extra oil in our vessels. We may have salvation and the baptism of the Holy Spirit yet still be lacking. The old wine of the Spirit is fine, but when it runs out, what will we do? The new wine is that fresh oil that will meet us at the point where our present cup runs dry. The Charismatic renewal is quickly running dry and becoming a tradition in many regards. The Holy Spirit is inviting us to receive this new wine of the Holy Spirit that will take us through the dark hours of trials and emptiness and into a time of great renewal.

Do you have what it takes to win this world for Christ? Do you burn with a passion for the lost? Are you still overtaken by a spirit of intercession and travail for those on their way to hell, weeping for their salvation, as maybe you once did? As you see lost souls walking down a drug-infested street on their way to destruction, are you gripped with compassion, or have you become satisfied with things as they are? If you have lost that sense of urgency for the lost, then it is only one of many signs that you need more of the Holy Spirit. Drink in the waters of the Holy Spirit until you are overcome with Him and His heart for the world.

If you have been touched by this renewal, don't get satisfied! Cry out for more! Let your cry always be, "More, more, more of Him!" Those with the mightiest anointing in their lives are not those who are satisfied with just a little bit of blessing. They want the whole package! Once you have tasted of the new wine, you should continually yearn for more, or you will become satisfied. Eventually this new season of refreshing will produce fruit. Fruit such as love for others, a deeper walk with God, and a burning passion for the lost will result in the greatest revival in history.

This new wine is much more than only being refreshed and full of joy. This is only the first phase of a much higher purpose than your own personal fulfillment and happiness. Your vessel is being restored and renewed in preparation for a greater anointing than you have ever known so that you will see the Great Commission accomplished in and through your life!

RECEIVING TO GIVE

Jesus said to them, "Fill the waterpots with water." And they filled them up to the brim (John 2:7).

There are those who want just enough of the Holy Spirit to bless themselves and their own churches or ministries. Then there are those who want more than enough to not only bless themselves but to have more than enough to give away to others. Jesus sent out the servants to fill the waterpots and then give away the wine. Most certainly they too wanted some of the wine, yet they filled those waterpots with enough to serve the other guests. It says that they filled those pots to the brim. You can't get more full than that. Their desire was not just to have enough for themselves but to serve the entire wedding party.

Jesus implemented the idea of receiving more than enough as He *commanded* them to *fill* the pots with water. The Holy Spirit is asking us to do the same: get full of Him until you are bubbling over with the new wine and have a more than adequate supply to give to others as well. This is the difference between someone who is a servant and someone who is self-serving.

This is why people will come forward for prayer two or three times in the same service until they are totally filled. It's not that they did not receive anything the first time, but they want as much as possible in order to be able to give some of it away. They are walking in obedience to Jesus' command to be filled. It grieves the Holy Spirit when someone receives and then puts down those who have not yet received, feeling superior due to an experience. This is the danger that must be avoided at all costs, so as not to quench the Holy Spirit. Humility is the fruit of a servant. We must become water fetchers, filling up to give out. Don't just come to receive a refreshing for yourself and let it stop there.

At what point can this fresh water of the Holy Spirit become a mighty anointing in us so that we give this blessing to others while continually being refilled? Some seem to be able to give away this blessing with ease, while others are still caught up in their own experience. The attitude of receiving to give is not a formula, but it must become an attitude of the heart.

> *And He said to them, "Draw some out now, and take it to the master of the feast." And they took it. When the master of the feast had tasted the water that was made wine, and did not know where it came from (but the servants who had drawn the water knew), the master of the feast called the bridegroom* (John 2:8-9).

These servants simply obeyed Jesus, and that is when the miracle took place. If you'll look carefully, the water miraculously turned to wine only when the servants began to "give away" the water to the master of the feast so he could taste it. It did not happen when they filled the waterpots with water. It took a greater act of faith to serve to the master of the feast the water that they hoped had become wine by the time he tasted it. These servants were most likely worried about losing their jobs. This was a test of their faith in Jesus.

If you have received a fresh filling of the water of the Spirit, that's a great start. You are like the guests who drank well. But after the party, the guests went home because they were only there to be served. Only the servants knew how and where to get a continual supply of the new wine. We need to receive with a servant's heart of giving. In this way, we will be given much more as the Holy Spirit knows our motives for receiving, and what we will do with it. God knows your heart, and He will give according to your need and your willingness to bless someone else with it.

As soon as you receive, find someone you can give to who is thirsty for a drink of the Holy Spirit. This will take a step of faith on your part as you may be thinking, *I don't have what it takes to give this out to others.* Actually, you're absolutely right, you don't. But the Holy Spirit working through you does. By faith in His ability to bless others, you can do it! These servants knew that there was only water in those pots, not wine. They knew that apart from a miracle of Jesus they were totally inadequate. The beauty behind all this is that Jesus does the miracles, and all we do is obey.

After I had begun to receive the new wine for myself, I felt nothing in particular. Yet as I began to give away what I believed I had received immediately afterward, the new wine of the Holy Spirit began to be poured out in churches and meetings everywhere we ministered. It would happen even before we got a chance to speak. The more we gave, the more we would also be refilled to give again. It has not stopped since. Whether in a large meeting or one on one with a friend, God is faithful to fill those who are hungry. Our job is to serve the drinks, and God will take care of the supply when it runs dry.

This anointing on our lives has considerably increased due to this principle. I truly believe that if I had not continued to serve others this blessing and stay hungry for more, I may very well have become confused and discouraged. My cup would eventually have run dry.

Apply this principle of giving and receiving to every area of your life. A giver takes on the very character of Christ, whose nature is to give. Jesus never said that it would be easier to be a servant instead of a guest, just that it would be more blessed.

I have shown you in every way, by laboring like this, that you must support the weak. And remember the words of the Lord Jesus, that He said, "It is more blessed to give than to receive" (Acts 20:35).

...For everyone to whom much is given, from him much will be required; and to whom much has been committed, of him they will ask the more (Luke 12:48).

CHAPTER 4

Keeping and Multiplying the New Wine

And when they ran out of wine, the mother of Jesus said to Him, "They have no wine" …His mother said to the servants, "Whatever He says to you, do it" (John 2:3,5).

A common concern among those who have tasted the new wine is how to keep it flowing and not lose it. Maybe you are not in an area where this blessing is occurring. You may feel that you have run dry. This is a very real and important concern, especially among workers who need to give it out. You need to get to the point where you learn to receive the new wine without always having to "import" it. Of course, if the outpouring of new wine is happening at your church it will be easier. But for the many others who are not so fortunate, there are other ways to keep the water flowing. You don't have to settle for staying dry while wishing for more. You must dig deep and develop your own source instead of always importing it from someone else's vineyard.

75

My wife and I had to face this problem immediately after receiving the new wine. We were scheduled to minister in different cities and countries and wanted to bless other Christians with what we had received. We were forced to learn rather quickly how to keep it flowing. How do you find it when there is no nearby source to draw from—especially when others earnestly want a refreshing from the Holy Spirit and expect you to be the water boy?

Awake, you drunkards, and weep; and wail, all you drinkers of wine, because of the new wine, for it has been cut off from your mouth (Joel 1:5).

FASTING

The guests who come to the wedding party on a full stomach will have a harder time receiving this wine because they are not thirsty for it. Also, the guests will not be able to appreciate the new wine as they are already temporarily satisfied with another source. On the other hand, those guests who have come on an empty stomach in anticipation of the new wine will feel the effects much more quickly and will be able to drink in much more than those who have lost their appetite. The effects of new wine on an empty stomach are certainly powerful.

The Bible alludes to fasting time and time again in regard to being filled with the new wine of the Holy Spirit. Only one chapter before the prophecy of the great outpouring of the Holy Spirit in Joel 2:28, we see a command to fast prior to the outpouring.

Consecrate a fast, call a sacred assembly; gather the elders and all the inhabitants of the land into the house of the Lord your God, and cry out to the Lord (Joel 1:14).

"Now, therefore," says the Lord, "Turn to Me with all your heart, with fasting and weeping, and with mourning." ...Who

knows if He will turn and relent, and leave a blessing behind Him—a grain offering and a drink offering for the Lord your God? (Joel 2:12,14)

When we obey God in this way there will be a response to our sincere and desperate prayers.

The Lord will answer and say to His people, "Behold, I will send you grain and new wine and oil, and you will be satisfied by them..." (Joel 2:19).

Fasting is one of the quickest ways to empty and clean out your vessel. In doing this you are actually allowing yourself to hunger for the things of God. This puts your whole being in a position that makes it easier for you to cooperate with what God has for you. Only those who hunger for more of Him will be filled. Fasting will cure spiritual apathy and cause hunger for the things of God to return. Fasting actually magnifies your sensitivity to the Holy Spirit by obliterating the flesh, which is the primary hindrance to receiving. This facilitates your mind, will, and emotions to be in total surrender to and communion with the Holy Spirit.

The 120 believers fasted and prayed in the Upper Room only days before the Holy Spirit was poured out on them in His fullness, much as we are experiencing today in the present move of God upon the Church. In essence, we deny ourselves when we fast in order to make room for the supernatural. This form of coming to the end of ourselves is the way of the cross. It is the ideal place for God to take over.

A church in a small town in France began to experience the new wine in January of 1994. This was the same month that the renewal really began to explode around the world. The spark that ignited the renewal in the French church occurred at the end of a ten-day corporate fast. Only months later did they discover that the same outpouring of the Holy Spirit was taking place in different countries and on different continents about the same time. It has not stopped since then.

Even after the disciples received the fullness of the Holy Spirit at Pentecost, they continued the pattern of prayer and fasting as the renewal continued to develop into an ever-increasing revival. Whenever they would prepare to go out on a new ministry venture, fasting was the prerequisite in order to be able to fully accomplish God's will in His strength and power and not their own. This was also the manner in which they handled crucial decisions within the church. They did not just take a vote, as many do today—they "took" a fast. This eliminated following their own human reasoning, which avoided many pitfalls and allowed the early Church to obey the will of God in many critical circumstances.

Are we truly willing to pay the price for a continued anointing and renewal, or are we satisfied with just a little blessing that eventually dies out? Men and woman with an agonizing hunger and desperation for more of God in this renewal will be the ones to spark the flames of revival from this renewal. This has been the pattern throughout the history of most revivals.

But the days will come when the bridegroom will be taken away from them; then they will fast in those days (Luke 5:35).

Jesus laid out this model for the disciples to receive the fullness of the Holy Spirit after His departure. In our days the Holy Spirit is again being poured out in great measure. Those willing to press in and pay any price will receive it all.

Fasting is one of the ways to press in and violently attack the carnality of our flesh. Often we have become old wineskins. We must allow God to break our wineskins and remake them into more solid and flexible vessels that can handle the new anointing without bursting. After we fall on the rock and are broken, only God can piece us back together.

Fasting prepares our wineskins to receive the new wine. Only two verses later Jesus explains to the disciples exactly why they will fast when He is taken away, and what the fast will produce:

And no one puts new wine into old wineskins; or else the new wine will burst the wineskins and be spilled, and the wineskins will be ruined. But new wine must be put into new wineskins, and both are preserved. And no one, having drunk old wine, immediately desires new; for he says, "The old is better" (Luke 5:37-39).

We are not advocating doing away with any trace of old wine teachings. Revelation from previous moves of the Spirit, such as faith, salvation, intercession, and so on are all examples of new wine that has matured into the old. Don't do away with the wisdom and maturity of the old, but also make room to embrace the new. It's really the wineskin that needs to be remade in order to be able to handle the new wine.

Some find it hard to flow with this new move because they are so used to the old ways and past moves of God. We need to give them their space and allow them time to adjust. Jesus even said in the previous verse that they would not "immediately" desire the new, hinting that given time, they may. Do not disregard the old wine or put down those who do not immediately desire to take part in the present move of the Holy Spirit. The wisdom of the old wine-skins, such as faith, for example, can help us channel this renewal into a greater outpouring until revival is the result. We must incor-porate the wisdom of the old to know how to make the best use of the new wine.

Ministries that have been operating under the old wine and receive the new will find that they will have an additional advantage. The effectiveness of the new anointing will be even greater when combined with the much needed experience, maturity, and integrity of the old. This combination will propel ministries into a deeper and more concentrated level of power.

If the anointing on your life is becoming stale and starting to leak out, strengthen your vessel through fasting. You will be able to preserve the new wine much longer and receive much more.

PRAISE AND WORSHIP

The wedding party is great, but people are wondering where the bride and the groom are. Then all of a sudden music fills the air. People begin to sing and dance in honor of the groom and his bride. When the music reaches its height, the newlyweds come out to present themselves to the guests they have invited. At this point, the celebration reaches its climax. What kind of wedding would this be if there was no music to set the atmosphere for the presentation of the bride and groom?

Another key to maintaining the new wine is praise and worship. Praise will usher in God's presence and more new wine. Christian leaders in several European countries have organized 24-hour praise celebrations called the "Tabernacle of David." I have assisted and ministered at some of these celebrations. I was literally recharged with an anointing of joy and power the whole time the praise was taking place. We had quite a breakthrough into the heavenly realm where Jesus is in His glory and is experiencing unspeakable joy. As continued praise and worship taps into this source, that concentrated joy and power in Heaven becomes manifested on earth.

Praise is going on 24 hours a day in Heaven. When we follow Heaven's pattern of praise and worship, the results are out of this world. We actually get a taste of what it is like in Heaven. When King David finally had the ark of the covenant returned from the hand of the Philistines, he was ecstatic. He sang, danced, and celebrated the return of the presence of the Lord (see 2 Sam. 6:12-16).

Many Christian leaders are beginning to sense the need to celebrate the return of the presence of the Lord in this new move of God. Previously they may have been spiritually dry, desperately awaiting this refreshing. Should we not also celebrate the restoration of God's presence in this renewal? Or will we take His presence for granted?

King David appointed Levites in the tabernacle to commemorate, thank, and praise the Lord God of Israel. In First Chronicles 16:4-6, David appointed Levites to offer nonstop praise with 24 groups of 12 singers to praise the Lord God. David set up a training system for singers and musicians training thousands during his lifetime that resulted in day and night worship for 33 years in front of the ark. That is one music group per hour, allowing for 24 hours a day of praise and worship. David copied the structure of praise and worship in Heaven's Kingdom. It is no wonder that the kingdom of Israel under King David was so powerful and prosperous. Praise actually maintained God's presence in the nation.

Christians in different countries touched by this renewal are doing exactly what King David did, and they are reaping the benefits. The results have been a constant outpouring of the Holy Spirit, especially when praise is done in conjunction with other local churches. Great damage is being done to the powers of darkness during these praise celebrations. Worship is penetrating into the dark clouds of evil that for too long have had great influence over whole communities and cities.

Believers are thanking God in one accord for His great joy and power with which He is renewing and restoring us. We need much more of this type of unity and corporate praise. This form of praise can be applied to an individual level inside your own home as well. David learned the secret power of praise as a young man. He played his harp to the disobedient King Saul and chased away tormenting spirits from him. How much more will we be blessed if we obediently apply praise to our own lives, ministries, and nations?

My wife and I often worship the Lord with praise and worship CDs. This allows for a continual flow of the river of God's presence to consume us. Even while conducting deliverance over a person we make sure to play some powerful praise music. This has often made the anointing much stronger and actually helped speed up the deliverance process. Demons become like fish out of water in this type of atmosphere and do not survive very well.

Churches that are experiencing much of this renewal make worship the highlight of the services. Even during the ministry sessions, which can last many hours into the night, worship is still taking place. For some churches this goes on six days a week. No wonder there is a higher concentration of God's presence in such places! In our own meetings, whether at home or overseas, we always give praise and worship a primary place. In this atmosphere we have seen the miraculous flow very easily and sinners have been converted in some of the darkest spiritual jungles of this world.

Leaders moving in this renewal have discovered the secret is not simply how to have the renewal in their own lives and churches. The secret really is what they did with it once they have it. Because of a lack of wisdom, many who receive this anointing let it die. Some churches have managed to become filling stations for many thirsty souls who travel long distances to drink at their source. Many of these churches are being propelled into worldwide ministries mostly because of the steps that the leadership is taking to make sure that the renewal does not just come and go. Their biggest concern is how not to stand in the way of the Holy Spirit—and above all how not to grieve Him. Ministries that will take the necessary steps to maintain renewal will continue to ride the wave all the way through to revival. The result is that history is being made. Since the renewal of 94 other revivals like the Brownsville Revival broke out shortly after the evangelist Steve Hill attended a renewal service. The move of God at Bethel church pastored by Bill Johnson is heavily influenced by praise and worship and renewal as well.

When we show the same awe and respect for the presence of God as King David did, He will stay around much longer. A "now I've got it" attitude that takes Him for granted, without a careful maintenance of His presence, will cause this renewal to slowly dry up. Kathryn Kuhlman knew this principle ever so well. In some of her meetings she used to cry out to the audience, "Please, don't grieve Him—He's all I have." She realized that once the Holy Spirit was offended, she could not minister to the people under that same anointing. Just the thought of God's presence leaving her even temporarily would put her in agony. King David thought that losing Him once was enough. He never again wanted the ark of God's presence to leave, and he did all he knew to keep it. So he praised and worshiped the Lord.

These praise celebrations are accelerating the presence of God from renewal to revival. My desire, along with that of many others, is that the lost will be touched by the overflow of this renewal as we nurture it and take the proper steps to ensure its growth.

TITHES

Such a grand wedding is not without cost. The guests are freely invited, yet the wine, the servants, the renting of the wedding area, etc., must be paid for. Somehow the basic needs of this wedding must be provided. The guests are expected to bring gifts to honor the bride and groom. With these provisions, the bride and groom, in turn, must also pay the servants who have been chosen and have willingly served. Their livelihood depends on it. Though they are mere waiters in the eyes of the guests, without them there would be no one to deliver and serve the new wine that has brought them so much joy. It is common courtesy to honor the bride and groom for freely inviting them to the celebration. The continuation of the party depends on it.

> *Honor the Lord with your possessions, and with the firstfruits of all your increase; so your barns will be filled with plenty. And your vats overflow with new wine* (Proverbs 3:9-10).

Yes, finances play a big role in the process of receiving more of this renewal and the blessings that come with it. This spiritual principle has not changed.

What are the firstfruits of all our increase that will unlock the door to the new wine? It is the giving of all our tithes and offerings, which is obviously not a suggestion on God's behalf, but a command. Some Christians have thought that giving in this way results only in receiving materially from God. In actuality, this type of obedience in giving will result in added spiritual blessing as well.

> *"Bring all the tithes into the storehouse, that there may be food in My house, and try Me now in this," says the Lord of hosts, "If I will not open for you the windows of heaven and pour out for you such blessing that there will not be room enough to receive it"* (Malachi 3:10).

This passage of Scripture is the most popular when it comes time to take up an offering. Let's take a deeper look at what it is really saying here. It may surprise you.

The first reason God gives us in Malachi for the tithes is so there may be food in God's house. Why would there be a need for food? It is to feed the priests who minister and live in the temple. The opening of the windows of Heaven applies to renewal falling from Heaven because of our obedience in this area. What else would you think would fall from Heaven? God wants to bless us so much spiritually that we will not have enough room to receive it. I believe that one of the manifestations of this will eventually be a great harvest of souls running into our churches where the presence of God is abounding; they will feed on the spiritual food from Heaven and pack out our buildings. This happens today in revivals in many third world countries where there simply is not enough room to hold all the people coming in. The result is often outdoor meetings.

Why are so many pastors and leaders today not only running out of the wine of the Holy Spirit but also lacking the finances in their ministries to even survive? Countless full-time ministers are getting second jobs or dropping out of ministry altogether because of lack of finances to feed themselves and their families. Churches often close down and congregations scatter as a result. Why is the devourer not being rebuked? Does God have anything to say to this problem? Yes, He does! This problem is not new—it arose in Nehemiah's day.

> *I also realized that the portions for the Levites had not been given them; for each of the Levites and the singers who did the work had gone back to his field. So I contended with the rulers, and said, "Why is the house of God forsaken?" And I gathered them together and set them in their place. Then all Judah brought the tithe of the grain and the new wine and the oil to the store-house* (Nehemiah 13:10-12).

God's people were not giving the Levites their portion, the tithe that provided the Levites' basic needs. The singers who did the work of caring for the temple of God's presence were forced to leave the temple and return to working "normal" jobs. In this way God's house was neglected. This would eventually result in God's spiritual and material blessing being withheld. This is what Nehemiah dreaded the most. The new wine, the oil, and the grain represented the physical as well as the spiritual blessing that would be manifested if God's people would obey the tithe.

Also, they were profaning the Sabbath by working on the day of rest. How many leaders and believers today do the same by over-working and never taking a day to rest, get renewed, and meditate on the Lord. We must realize the implications here! We must take care of His Kingdom and obey Him in the little things before we start wondering where the anointing and joy has gone. These are some of the reasons why many ministers and workers are "burned out."

The tithes were strictly for the personal needs of the priests and their food supply. The tithe was never to be used for the temple itself!

> *Then the Lord spoke to Moses, saying, "Speak thus to the Levites, and say to them: 'When you take from the children of Israel the tithes which I have given you from them as your inheritance, then you shall offer up a heave offering of it to the Lord, a tenth of the tithe.' ... Therefore you shall say to them: 'When you have lifted up the best of it, then the rest shall be accounted to the Levites as the produce of the threshing floor and as the produce of the winepress. You may eat it any place, you and your households, for it is your reward for your work in the tabernacle of meeting'"* (Numbers 18:25-26;30-31).

Again, we can clearly see from this passage and many others that the tithe is to be primarily designated to those who are in full-time ministry to care for God's house and the continuation of the presence of the Lord. Even the priests were to tithe a tenth of the tithes they received. If they did not they were profaning the Lord's house and would be worthy of death. It was that serious.

Why is it that today the tithe is used for the church, the rent, building programs, and everything else except keeping ministers of the gospel in full-time ministry? Imagine how many hundreds of thousands of pastors, evangelists, missionaries, and other workers could be thrust out into their full-time ministerial calling if the tithe was properly appropriated today! It may sound revolutionary and too radical a change, but it is the pattern that has been laid for us. This is where the blessing lies. In total obedience to what the Holy Spirit is revealing to His people in this move today.

Some may try to say that we are not under the law and that tithing is from the law simply because it is in the Old Testament. This is a weak attempt to try and find any excuse to not obey God in this area. Actually, Abraham was the first to pay tithes to Melchizidek, the high priest, *before* the law or any other legal requirements were ever introduced. He did it by faith as unto the Lord. Those who would call this legalism are actually themselves caught up in a legalism concerning tithes that does not exist in the Bible. We are to live by faith as Abraham did. Out of his faith and generosity he gave his tithe of all the spoils he had acquired during war. Abraham is the father of faith and we are saved by faith. We must do no less in the area of the tithes because without faith it is impossible to please God (see Heb. 11:6).

*And he blessed him and said: "Blessed be Abram of God Most High, Possessor of heaven and earth; and blessed be God Most High, who has delivered your enemies into your hand." And he gave him a tithe of **all** (Genesis 14:19-20).*

OFFERINGS

The other aspect of giving financially is in the offerings. If the tithe is used solely for the ministers then there will be a major need for offerings in order to sustain the ministry expenses. How in the world can there be enough offerings to cover all the costs of running a church or ministry? There needs to be a massive increase in the giving of offerings for this to be possible. In most cases the offerings would have to be even greater than the tithes as many ministry expenses are greater than the expenses of the workers. Somehow, the proper concept of tithes and offerings has been distorted and the Church has been robbed of God's blessing in many ways. What is the proper biblical basis for changing the problem into a blessing?

> *And Moses spoke to all the congregation of the children of Israel, saying, "This is the thing which the Lord commanded, saying: 'Take from among you an offering to the Lord. Whoever is of a willing heart, let him bring it as an offering to the Lord…'"* **…Then everyone came whose heart was stirred, and everyone whose spirit was willing, and they brought the Lord's offering for the work of the tabernacle of meeting, for all its service,** *and for the holy garments. They came, both men and women, as many as had a willing heart…"* (Exodus 35:4-5;21-22).

Notice carefully that those of a willing heart were the ones who were to give their offerings. No guilt trips or manipulation when taking the offering. Having a willing heart was the prerequisite here. Also, the people were *stirred* to give. Do you suppose it was Moses alone who could stir all these people to give? I believe that the Holy Spirit was the One who stirred them with a zeal for the presence of the Lord in their midst. The presence of the Lord will change our hearts and make us willing to give with thankfulness simply for the love of His presence in our midst.

I know of churches that have been transformed by this renewal and have taken this principle of tithes and offerings very seriously, as it was intended. The result is that they are putting more people into full-time ministry and on the mission field than they could ever have imagined. Also, they are growing by leaps and bounds—and so is the presence of God in their churches. They report being tremendously blessed on all sides and do not lack in any good thing in order to fulfill the vision God has given them.

> *...And they brought the Lord's offering for the work of the tabernacle of meeting, for all its service and for the holy garments* (Exodus 35:21).

Let us not forget that the offerings need to cover the ministry expenses. What was the result when the people of God obeyed first in the tithe and then in offerings? They had more than enough to fulfill God's purposes! Many ministers and ministries have a true calling and vision yet fail to fully carry it out due to lack of finances and the blessing of God. The result of such giving in Moses' day was incredible.

> *And they received from Moses all the offerings which the children of Israel had brought for the work of the service of making the sanctuary. So they continued bringing to him freewill offerings every morning. Then all the craftsmen who were doing all the work of the sanctuary came, each from the work he was doing, and they spoke to Moses, saying, "The people bring much more than enough for the service of the work which the Lord commanded us to do." So Moses gave a commandment, and they caused it to be proclaimed throughout the camp, saying, "Let neither man nor woman do any more work for the offering of the sanctuary." And the people were restrained from bringing, for the material they had was sufficient for all the work to be done— indeed too much* (Exodus 36:3-7).

These are the kinds of problems we need today so that God's Kingdom is advanced and more of God's "Levites" can serve Him as they are called! The Lord is greatly pleased when His people are sensitive to the stirring of His Spirit and have the same willingness to see God's will accomplished through their giving.

The result was not just physical but also spiritual—the presence and glory of a mighty visitation of God! We too can obey that stirring and reap the same results.

> *Then the cloud covered the tabernacle of meeting, and the glory of the Lord filled the tabernacle. And Moses was not able to enter the tabernacle of meeting, because the cloud rested above it, and the glory of the Lord filled the tabernacle. ...For the cloud of the Lord was above the tabernacle by day, and fire was over it by night, in the sight of all the house of Israel, throughout all their journeys* (Exodus 40:34-35,38).

If we will let it, the present move of God can so affect our lives that we will be a testimony of God's presence in every area. This includes fasting, praise, and giving. Our willingness to obey in these areas will greatly contribute to the continued anointing of the new wine in our lives. We give our all and God gives His all. Now that is a good exchange!

> *Ho! Everyone who thirsts, come to the waters; and you who have no money, come, buy and eat. Yes, come, buy wine and milk* (Isaiah 55:1).

CHAPTER 5

Manifestations of New Wine

When the master of the feast had tasted the water that
was made wine, and did not know where it came from (but
the servants who had drawn the water knew), the master
of the feast called the bridegroom.... This beginning of
signs Jesus did in Cana of Galilee, and manifested His
glory; and His disciples believed in Him (John 2:9,11).

As the master of the feast wondered where the new wine he had tasted came from, some Christians are asking the same questions—before ever tasting the new wine. The seemingly new manifestations are causing the concern because they are not like anything many of us have seen before. God often uses foolish things to confound our human wisdom (see 1 Cor. 1:27).

During these seasons of special visitation from the Holy Spirit, some peculiar manifestations appear to be occurring. I don't want to put too much emphasis on manifestations, yet this subject needs to be addressed as it may leave some of you with a big question mark. I don't want manifestations to hinder you from being touched by this renewal.

Many Christians hold to the tradition that the Holy Spirit is always a "gentleman" and will never force anything upon us without our consent. However, the Scriptures seem to show quite the opposite! We will look at some examples shortly. It may very well be that many of us have never seen a genuine outpouring of the fullness of the Holy Spirit in operation as it happened on the day of Pentecost.

Often when someone manifests in an unusual fashion, people tend to label it all as demonic. The problem is that most people have only seen demonic manifestations, and so they rely on this past experience instead of the discernment of the Holy Spirit. Is it not possible that a believer can be so overcome with the Spirit of God that he or she could be overcome with certain manifestations? Our natural bodies can only handle so much of the supernatural.

When someone gets electrocuted, his body cannot help but manifest the power going through him. But that does not mean that electricity is always a negative thing. Of course there will always be those hungry for attention who may try to fake a manifestation and act it out in the flesh or under their own inspiration. That should not be our primary concern. Anyone can fake speaking in tongues, falling to the floor, or prophesying. But this should not stop others from reacting in these ways when the Spirit of God is truly affecting them. Basically, we should not throw out the baby with the bath water.

It's OK to admit that at times manifestations look strange or that we don't quite understand them. Yet some may feel uncomfortable or even afraid when they occur. Most fear is caused by a lack of knowledge. People are naturally afraid of the unknown. Once there is some understanding, fear subsides, leaving room for the peace of God. Just because you may not understand something does not mean that it is not of God! Isn't it possible that we may not have seen it all?

When I first saw the manifestations in renewal, I was tempted to leave and judge the move as being out of order. It was way beyond the norm and seemed to be out of control—at least out of my control or the control of anyone in the meeting. My mind told me, *Be careful.* So I prayed and asked the Holy Spirit to give me some discernment as to what was really going on. As I did, I felt such a peace, and the voice of the Holy Spirit telling me, "Don't judge what you do not understand but just continue to stay and receive!" The Holy Spirit will guide us into all truth. When you are sensitive to the Holy Spirit, you will know if what is happening is from God or not. The Word of God commands us to judge all things by their fruits, not simply by our own experiences or lack of them (see Matt. 12:33).

We will now take a deeper look at some of the manifestations occurring in this renewal. Some of these have direct biblical references while others are implied in the Scriptures.

Falling

Often people will fall to the floor without anyone laying hands on them in prayer. Falling has occurred since Bible days, yet has been more common among Charismatic and Pentecostal circles. It is happening much more frequently in the present move. It is one of the most common of all the phenomena taking place.

Many times when the Holy Spirit instructs me to pray for people en masse without touching them, many bodies are flung to the floor by the power of God. At times there are not enough people to catch them, though they are never hurt when it is the Holy Spirit spontaneously at work. We always arrange for catchers when it is in our control, yet the Holy Spirit sometimes allows people to fall with no forewarning. Even during a simple sermon this has occurred.

As I mentioned earlier, we can be so consumed with the presence of God and so engaged in a sweet communion with the Holy Spirit that our bodies become weak as they are overcome by God's power. In this stage, the person may feel very light and filled with incredible peace and joy. The person will not necessarily want to be helped back up too soon, as it could hinder what God may be doing at the moment. During my experience in the Upper Room in Jerusalem, I had the options to resist falling and to get back up, yet I felt so renewed and confident that the Holy Spirit was at work that I did not want to hinder what God was doing with me.

There are numerous biblical accounts of people falling when the presence of God was powerfully present. Just open your Bible or a concordance and look up the words *fall, fell,* or even *lying stunned on the ground.* You will find many instances in both the Old and New Testaments when God's presence was particularly near that falling occurred.

When Paul (who was still called Saul at the time) was apprehended on the road to Damascus and fell to the ground, I doubt that he was faking this experience! (see Acts 9:3-9.) It does not appear that the Holy Spirit was a "gentleman" in this situation, or in many others we read about in the Word of God.

When Judas and the soldiers came to arrest Jesus, they, too, had an interesting encounter when Jesus revealed who He was in His power (see John 18:3-6). There is a sense of humility when we fall down in the presence of the Almighty God. We are humbled and He is exalted as we recognize His power. This is what happened to the soldiers who came to arrest Jesus on the night that Judas betrayed Him.

In the vision that resulted in the Book of Revelation, John spoke of his angelic encounter saying,

> *And when I saw Him,* **I fell at His feet as dead**... (Revelation 1:17).

Whether or not this happened for the exact same reason is not the question. What we do know is that the falling occurred as a direct response to God's power.

Countless revivals throughout history have experienced falling. Jonathan Edwards, the main instrument and theologian of "The Great Awakening" in America (1726-1760), said in the account of the "Revival of Religion in Northhampton":

> Many have had their affections raised far beyond what they had seen before; and there were some instances of persons lying in a sort of trance, remaining perhaps for a whole twenty-four hours motionless, and with their senses locked up, but in the meantime under strong imaginations, as though they went to heaven and had there a vision of glorious and delightful objects. It was a frequent thing to see outcries, fainting, conversions, and such like, both with distress, and also admiration and joy. It was not the manner here to hold meetings all night, nor was it common to continue them until very late in the night, but it was pretty often so, that there were some so affected and their bodies so overcome that they could not go home, but were obligated to stay all night where they were.[1]

As we can see here, these experiences are not new to Church history, only to those who have never heard or encountered such things. When sensing God's presence pushing me down, I find it much better to "go with the flow" and let God have His way. Something is imparted to us when we allow Him to have His way with us. For some people, it is not even a choice as they are forced to the ground by God's power. We have seen this in the Scriptures.

Charles Finney (1792-1875) was also one of the most powerful revivalists in history. In one account he wrote:

> At a country place named Sodom, in the state of New York, Finney gave one address in which he described the condition of Sodom before God destroyed it. "I had not spoken in this strain for more than a quarter of an hour," says he, "when an awful solemnity seemed to settle upon them; the congregation began to fall from their seats in every direction, and cried for mercy. If I had a sword in my hand, I could not have cut them down as fast as they fell. Nearly the whole congregation were either on their knees or prostrate. I should think, in less than two minutes from the shock that fell upon them everyone prayed who was able to speak at all."[2]

Falling may take place in a variety of spiritual circumstances. In the text of Finney's account, it was accompanied by a holy fear and a somewhat forced and sudden prostration. At the present we are seeing most of the falling toward renewing, blessing, anointing, and revelation. Many people find their "floor time" with God as a time of rest in the Lord when they are refreshed.

In past years I used to have trouble with the issue of falling. When we allow our fears to go and totally surrender to what the Holy Spirit wants, we can be blessed through the experience of falling under the power of God. These are not things we should attempt to fabricate or make ourselves do by habit, but if it does happen, don't worry, be happy!

SHAKING

Shaking is one of the phenomena that most seems to concern many people. At times it can appear almost violent and therefore be difficult to understand. It is very similar to someone being plugged into a strong electrical current—this shaking can involve all sorts of bodily contortions. The manifestations are not just for show. They are there for a reason and are evidence of something else, something much more powerful than meets the eye. It is an overflow of what is really happening inside the person. Since we have been ministering and traveling to different countries under this anointing, we have noticed some similarities with this manifestation that will help shed some light on this subject.

On different occasions, as the Lord leads, we will have special altar calls for people to come forward not just to be renewed and filled with joy, but specifically to receive a special anointing that the Holy Spirit is wanting to disperse upon His people for service. Often those who shake may be receiving an anointing, which tends to be in the area of the prophetic, intercession, other revelatory gifts, and/or evangelism. It is not limited to these anointings, but these are the most common anointings we are seeing that are accompanied by shaking.

These people may have already been operating in a certain gift, yet receive a renewed and increased anointing in that area. At the same time these people may have never operated in a certain gift and may now be receiving a special anointing to do so. Some people who have never prophesied in their lives will begin to do so with great accuracy when the Spirit of God comes upon them. This has happened even with little children.

The fact that certain manifestations are often followed by an increase in the anointing indicates a much stronger level of power in these gifts than the person may have experienced previously. It does not mean that every time a person moves in one of these gifts that he or she will shake. Other people may receive the same gift with the same anointing and never shake at all. It all depends on the Holy Spirit.

We are not to seek after manifestations! We need only to seek after more of God, His presence, and His anointing on our lives. Whatever happens after that is up to Him. No one should ever try to copy or mimic a certain manifestation to try to look anointed. That is foolishness because a manifestation is not any indication or proof that someone has received an anointing. We discover the effects by the fruit that will follow.

In the Old Testament, Daniel received a vision that was a prophetic revelation of what was to come, and he began to tremble. What exactly caused his trembling we may not totally understand. What we do know is that after his breakthrough, as the anointing for intercession overcame his prayers, he trembled in some way (see Dan. 10:11). The prophetic gift is also often intertwined with intercession. Daniel moved in the realm of intercession as he prayed and fasted for 21 days. This shaking may also come upon others receiving an anointing for intercession. Any of these gifts can come upon any believer whom God chooses. Ministers who flow with the prophetic gift find it a complement to their ministry. We need to be open to these things and not limit the Holy Spirit.

My heart within me is broken; because of the prophets; all my bones shake, I am like a drunken man, and like a man whom wine has overcome, because of the Lord, and because of His holy words (Jeremiah 23:9).

So shaking does not automatically mean a person is receiving one of these gifts, but that can be the case. God is raising up more and more men and women who will move in the gifts of prophecy and thus greatly edify the Body of Christ in these last days. In this move of God, "shaking prophecies" are becoming more frequent. A person in this state will begin to shake intensely and prophesy at the same time with exceptional boldness and force.

My wife often receives prophetic dreams and visions. After she received a renewed anointing in this area, the prophetic word originating from a prophetic vision or dream began, at times, to be accompanied by intense shaking right before she was to give a prophetic word. There have been many instances, especially during the beginning of this renewal, when I was alone in prayer and the mighty presence of the Lord came upon me very strongly as He revealed more of Himself to me. Then I begin to shake under this anointing. These have been precious moments with the Holy Spirit. It is a shame that anyone would attempt to fake experiences that they may once have had. Simply receive more of Jesus and don't get into emotionalism trying to relive a certain moment through a manifestation.

No wonder even the Israelites were afraid of the presence of God. They would not go near the mountain where His presence was. Instead they chose Moses to go (see Deut. 5:5; Heb. 12:18-21). The Scriptures tell us that the demons believe and also tremble when God is in their midst (see James 2:19). On some occasions when someone is receiving deliverance they may shake. People who purposely go into churches to disrupt the meeting through witchcraft or other occult activities can also be found shaking and in fear as they are overpowered by the presence of God. These people then realize that they have walked into the wrong building! As I mentioned earlier, we are seeing shaking in the present renewal mostly related to the anointing of God empowering a person. Jonathan Edwards also wrote:

Neither a negative or a positive judgment should be based on the manifestations alone because the Scripture gives us no such rule.[3]

John White also wrote that:

Manifestations, while they may be a blessing, are no guarantee of anything. Their outcome depends on the mysterious traffic between God and our spirits. Your fall and your shaking may be a genuine expression of the power of the Spirit resting on you. But the Spirit may not benefit you in the least if God does not have His way with you, while someone who neither trembles nor falls may profit greatly.[4]

DRUNK IN THE SPIRIT

Others mocking said, "They are full of new wine." But Peter, standing up with the eleven, raised his voice and said to them, "Men of Judea and all who dwell in Jerusalem, let this be known to you, and heed my words. For these are not drunk, as you suppose, since it is only the third hour of the day. But this is what was spoken by the prophet Joel" (Acts 2:13-16).

There is a difference between having a little joy and being drunk in the Spirit. The 120 newly filled believers in the Upper Room were definitely reacting in a drunken manner as the Scriptures in Acts clearly indicate. They were accused of being drunk because they were acting like drunks. There is no mystery hidden in this passage. In order to be accused of drunkenness they most certainly manifested laughing, falling, singing, strange speech, and great boldness without restraint as drunks are known to do.

The Bible tells us to be filled with the wine of the Holy Spirit, which has effects in the spiritual realm that are similar to the physical effects of real wine.

And do not be drunk with wine, in which is dissipation; but be filled [continuously filled] *with the Spirit, speaking to one another in psalms and hymns and spiritual songs, singing and making melody in your heart to the Lord* (Ephesians 5:18-19).

The big difference is that worldly drunkenness is sinful and leads to destruction while spiritual drunkenness is holy and leads to life more abundant. In this passage, singing to the Lord is shown as a source of being filled with the new wine of the Spirit.

When we were assisting in a communion service in Europe, the spirit of joy came upon my wife. She burst out in laughter and began rolling on the floor. Then two other ladies began to act similarly, butting people with their heads. Practically everyone whom they bumped into was also overcome with this joy. One person abounding with this joy can become contagious—it will quickly spread. This may very well have been the case after the day of Pentecost.

In many of our meetings people have often become so drunk in the Spirit that they have had to be carried out of the meeting long after the crowds have gone. When these people have come alone to the meeting, we try to get them designated drivers. This joy is not "casual"; it is the most powerful joy in the world. It is the joy that exists in Heaven. This is the joy of experiencing the fullness of the presence of God. The testimonies of people under the influence of heavenly wine are wonderful. Many discover the love of God in a new way. Others are relieved as heavy burdens are lifted off them. Still others find themselves healed both physically and emotionally during a time of drunkenness in the Spirit.

In a meeting in France, the Lord told me to call people up for prayer but not to touch them or come near them. He instructed me to just watch. People came up with their hands raised to Heaven. As on as they reached a certain area in the front of the building, these Christians instantly dropped to the floor as if lightning had struck them. Many were drunk in the Spirit. These were the same people who had to be carried out of the building after midnight. The awe of God fell upon that meeting. Souls were converted, and many healings and miracles took place.

FIRE

Then there appeared to them divided tongues, as of fire, and one sat upon each of them. And they were all filled with the Holy Spirit and began to speak with other tongues, as the Spirit gave them utterance (Acts 2:3-4).

The fire of the Holy Spirit is not mere symbolism but a sobering reality. God is restoring the fullness of what we read in the Scriptures and what literally took place in the Book of Acts.

My wife and I have often experienced the fire of the Holy Spirit, especially since this renewal occurred. At times our hands will become very hot, as if burning. This is then accompanied by a special anointing to heal. Others experiencing this may feel intense heat all over their body. For example, the first time this heat came on my hands I laid them on a man with an ulcer. It immediately burned up the ulcer until it totally disappeared. The man could also feel the intense heat burning it up.

On another occasion my wife's hands became so hot that she laid them on me in hopes of diminishing the burning heat. When she did this, that same fire came upon me. These anointings can be imparted to others as the Holy Spirit leads.

The verse above mentions divided tongues, as of fire. Obviously this manifestation is very similar to real fire. This fire cannot be seen, though there have been accounts of men and women of God who have actually seen it with their natural eyes. Though it cannot be seen, it can be felt. It also will burn away sickness and disease.

I indeed baptize you with water unto repentance, but He who is coming after me is mightier than I, whose sandals I am not worthy to carry. He will baptize you with the Holy Spirit and fire. His winnowing fan is in His hand, and He will thoroughly clean out His threshing floor, and gather His wheat into the barn; but He will burn up the chaff with unquenchable fire (Matthew 3:11-12).

There is a baptism of fire that is not the same as being baptized in water or the baptism of the Holy Spirit as we know it today. Fire either purifies or destroys. It is often referred to as a destructive fire that will be reserved in judgment for those who reject Christ. In the positive use of the term, the fire of God can cause a purging process and heal our physical bodies, burning away disease. The term "fired up for God," which is widely used in Pentecostal/Charismatic circles, may have derived its origin from this experience. We need to see more Christians being baptized with the fire of God, burning with a passion for souls, and destroying sin and sickness wherever they go. This fire can only come from the Holy Spirit. We must not be satisfied with only speaking in other tongues. We must go further and seek the full Pentecost experience that involves everything the early Church had.

For too long, "Spirit-filled" Christians have limited the baptism of the Holy Spirit to only speaking in other tongues. We need to be truly baptized—totally immersed in the Holy Spirit—until we have the fullness of Him. Only then will we be totally transformed and produce fruit that remains.

Prior to the day of Pentecost, the 72 disciples who were sent to cast out demons and heal the sick still had results (see Luke 10:1-18).

Yet they only possessed a small portion of the Holy Spirit, not the fullness. They are similar to many of us in our day who may have seen some results but are not satisfied with only a portion. Let us press in until we have that fullness that the Scriptures promise for all believers.

BLINDED AND UNABLE TO EAT

Another manifestation that is not mentioned very often is that of becoming blind or mute by the Holy Spirit. When Paul was on his mission to persecute the early Church, he was confronted by the power of God and fell to the ground blind and unable to eat.

> *So he trembled and astonished, said, "Lord, what do you want me to do?"...Then Saul arose from the ground and when his eyes were opened he saw no one. But they led him by the hand and brought him into Damascus. And he went three days without sight, and neither ate nor drank* (Acts 9:6,8-9).

In Europe, I met a young man from a Bible school in Switzerland at a national celebration of praise called "The Tabernacle of David." It consisted of 24 hours of nonstop praise on a New Year's Eve. This young man has been touched by this move of the Spirit as his Bible school was in a time of great visitation. He explained to all of us how he has been blinded by the Holy Spirit for over seven weeks when the Holy Spirit started to move in such power. During this season it was often that he could not speak unless it was to utter a prophetic word. That night, while playing the keyboard on one of the worship teams, he prophesied about the renewal that was occurring at the time. The message was that God is using seemingly foolish things to confound the wise men of our day who scoff at the idea that God could or would do such things today.

We cannot afford to limit what the Holy Spirit can and is doing in this end-time outpouring. The moment we think we have God all figured out, He will confound our minds with something new that we may not understand.

> *And Zecharias said to the angel, "How shall I know this? For I am an old man, and my wife is well advanced in years." …**But behold, you will be mute and not able to speak** until the day these things take place, because you did not believe my words which will be fulfilled in their own time." …**But when he came out, he could not speak to them;** and they perceived that he had seen a vision in the temple, for he beckoned to them and remained speechless (Luke 1:18,20,22).*

Zacharias doubted God's ability to bless him with a son in his old age. The result was that God used this experience to confound his human wisdom and those who heard about this. These types of manifestations are signs to the Body of Christ that God's wisdom is higher than man's wisdom.

> *For it is written: "I will destroy the wisdom of the wise, and bring to nothing the understanding of the prudent"* (1 Corinthians 1:19).

The idea that the Holy Spirit is always a gentleman and would never do anything to offend and shock us seems to be quickly changing for many. Whether this is really true depends on what your idea of what a perfect gentleman is.

On his way to kill David, King Saul began to prophesy when he came near the prophets. He did this naked for 24 hours day and night! (see 1 Sam. 19) He must have been thoroughly embarrassed and humiliated. I don't think he volunteered to do that. His intent that day was to murder David, not to prophesy. Paul's experience when he was knocked to the ground by God's power and then blinded was not gentleman-like either. The prophet Daniel could not help but tremble in the Lord's presence after his vision of events that were to come (see Dan. 10:11).

God wants to show this generation that He is in control and can do what He wants to do, when He wants and how He wants, without our permission. God is trying to humble us so that we can be fully usable in His hands. It is often said, "God offends the mind to reveal the heart."

One pastor who has been used to spark renewal asked God why He was bringing so much renewal to certain churches. God answered him by saying that He was looking for a people who were willing to look publicly foolish for the honor of His name. Are we willing to play the fool if need be for His glory if the Holy Spirit desires us to do so?

DISCERNING THE SPIRITS

If a kingdom is divided against itself, that kingdom cannot stand. And if a house is divided against itself, that house cannot stand. And if Satan has risen up against himself, and is divided, he cannot stand, but has an end (Mark 3:24-26).

Is every single manifestation that occurs in a move of God a sign of God's blessing? No! In any move of the Spirit of God upon a people, there will always be some people manifesting who are not doing so under the inspiration of the Holy Spirit. Once we have settled this in our minds, we can discern what is happening. If your spirit is sensitive to the Holy Spirit, you'll know the difference between what is of God and what is not. It is the same as when someone blurts out a prophecy that does not agree with your spirit. Just because someone blows it in prophecy does not mean we do away with all prophecy. We just need proper discernment. First

Corinthians 12:10 mentions a spiritual gift called the discerning of spirits. Leaders in the church especially need to have this gift! This will enable them to make sure things are running smoothly and Jesus is being glorified.

How can we recognize what is of the Holy Spirit and what is not?

> *Beloved, do not believe every spirit, but test the spirits, whether they are of God; because many false prophets have gone out into the world.* **By this you know the Spirit of God: Every spirit that confesses that Jesus Christ has come in the flesh is of God, and every spirit that does not confess that Jesus Christ has come in the flesh is not of God** (1 John 4:1-3).

First of all, if the person ministering exalts Jesus, the Holy Spirit will be the One who will come in response to his or her prayers. The enemy will never purposely exalt Jesus but only slander His name. When we are ministering with a heart that wants to exalt Jesus, we can trust that God will be working in the life of the person for whom we are praying.

The next question we may want to ask is: Is the manifestation God's blessing and renewal, empowerment, and anointing for service, or is it a power encounter in which an area of darkness has been exposed? Most of the shaking in this present move of God has to do with empowerment for service. Spiritual gifts of intercession, prophecy, healing, pastoral care, evangelism, and other such gifts are being imparted with great power to prepare God's people for the coming revival. The joy and laughter we mentioned earlier are good signs that God is restoring His people for the times ahead!

If the manifestation is because an area of darkness has been exposed, this calls for repentance for the sin that may have opened the door. This may even need to be followed up with deliverance. If so, it is wise to perform deliverance away from the main meeting room and in another nearby room, depending on the intensity and length of time the deliverance may take. If the person is performing wild manifestations for attention's sake on a continual basis, then proper discernment and pastoral intervention should be used.

CHECK OUT THE FRUIT

The biblical way to judge these manifestations is to examine the fruit they are producing. Any other standard of judging is unbiblical and leads to becoming a critical skeptic. By doing this we make ourselves a judge, thus taking the place of the true Judge in Heaven. To judge is to make a final decision concerning a person or a matter. The Pharisees made a judgment, or a final decision, concerning Jesus despite the great things He did and the fruit He produced. They made a final decision that He was not the Messiah for whom they were waiting. Even after He rose again when the angel rolled away the stone and the Roman guards dropped to the ground as dead men, the Pharisees chose not to believe. Instead they bribed the guards to say that Jesus' body was stolen despite the unquestionable evidence that He was raised (see Matt. 28:2-4;11-15).

We too must be careful not to make a final decision against this move lest we also miss this time of divine visitation for which we have been waiting. We must be wise and let God make a final decision concerning a manifestation—or anything else for that matter. Look for the fruit. Is Jesus really being glorified or not?

So far, from testimonies around the world and from our own personal experience in this renewal, people are falling in love with Jesus all over again in a whole new way. People are being healed and restored in every area. Ministers and believers are being renewed and healed of past scars and deep wounds in their personal lives and ministries. Many are receiving a call and anointing to be used in His service. We are noticing much humility and respect among Christians and leaders touched by the current renewal. This is producing the fruit of love and reconciliation which is promoting unity among God's people across denominational lines.

Barriers that have kept people from advancing with God are being broken. Physical and emotional healings, as well as deliverance from demonic oppression, are on the increase. A spirit of intercession for the unsaved is coming upon many in this renewal. A large number of backslidden Christians are returning to the Lord and to the local church. Those flowing and advancing in this renewal are receiving a fresh fire and boldness to evangelize, which is accelerating and becoming contagious!

You cannot argue with the fruit I have just described to you. These are only some of the fruits of this renewal. All the signs, wonders, phenomena, revelations, and manifestations are great, yet only secondary to the fruit of love. Many people who have been touched by this move say that what has convinced and changed them the most is the love they are experiencing from God and their brothers and sisters in Christ. It is refreshing to hear Christians talk about this love, which often has not been in the church, but is now being awakened. What are some of the signs of this love?

Love suffers long and is kind; love does not envy; love does not parade itself, is not puffed up; does not behave rudely, does not seek its own, is not provoked, thinks no evil; does not rejoice in iniquity, but rejoices in the truth; bears all things, believes all things, hopes all things, endures all things. Love never fails. But whether there are prophecies, they will fail; whether there are tongues, they will cease; whether there is knowledge, it will vanish away....And now abide faith, hope, love, these three; but the greatest of these is love (1 Corinthians 13:4-8,13).

Look for and believe God to bear this kind of fruit. It will speak more of what God is doing in a person's life than just outward manifestations.

ENDNOTES

1. Jonathan Edwards, *The Works of Jonathan Edwards, Volume One, Account of Revival of Religion in Northhampton 1740-42* (Carlisle, PA: Banner of Truth Trust, 1974).

2. Rev. C.G. Finney, *The Character, Claims And Practical Workings of Freemasonry* (Western Tract and Book Society, 1869).

3. Charles Finney, *The Distinguishing Marks of a Work of the Spirit of God* (Diggory Press, re-printed March 1, 2007).

4. John White, *When the Spirit Comes With Power* (Downers Grove, IL: InterVarsity Press, 1987), 81-82.

CHAPTER 6

Falling in Love

We love Him because He first loved us (1 John 4:19).

Let him kiss me with the kisses of his mouth—for your love is better than wine (Song of Solomon 1:2).

Let us be glad and rejoice and give Him glory, for the marriage of the Lamb has come, and His wife has made herself ready (Revelation 19:7).

There is an aspect of this wedding feast that is even more important than the manifestations, the gifts and offerings, who was invited, who was out of order, and more. The love relationship between the bride and the groom must be at the center of everything else that happens. If this is not the case then the celebration is in vain. What is the celebration really about anyway? Is it not the fact that a new love relationship between the bride and the groom has begun and the guests are invited to share in that joy?

THE LAW OF LOVE

Many "brides" marry out of convenience—to have their needs met and so on. How many Christians have come into a relationship with Jesus Christ out of convenience, yet never really know Him? The heart of any marriage is love. In fact, love is not really to be considered a choice; it is a requirement for the bride if she is to truly know the groom in his fullness and accomplish her destiny with him. Surely the bride can communicate this love to her family and friends who she has invited as guests to the party. But if she does not enter into a true love relationship with the groom eventually this love will wane.

Once married, the ability of a bride to fully express that love to those around her will depend on her ability to receive and love the groom. If this is not the case it will be evident that her marriage relationship is damaged, and this will affect her other relationships. This is the most serious law affecting the bride's success with the groom—it must never be broken.

"Teacher, which is the great commandment in the law?" Jesus said to him, "'You shall love the Lord your God with all your heart, with all your soul, and with all your mind.' This is the first and great commandment. And the second is like it: 'You shall love your neighbor as yourself.' On these two commandments hang all the Law and the Prophets" (Matthew 22:36-40).

The entire Bible from cover to cover is based on this one law of love. Yes, Christians are still under the law in this regard. For some reason, this love relationship slowly fades away for many of God's people. As time goes on they end up merely going through the motions. This tragedy stops the flow of renewal because love is at the root of every renewal. When that love relationship has grown cold the renewal stagnates. When this love atmosphere grows it will eventually give birth to a soul-winning revival.

How can you obey the second commandment to love your neighbor as yourself if you have not obeyed the first command to love the Lord your God with all your heart, mind, soul, and strength? You must obey the first commandment and thus go to the Source of love if you ever expect to give love. This is renewal. People often say that if this renewal were a true move of God then there should immediately be large masses of people receiving salvation. That is a wrong notion. Renewal is not the same thing as evangelism. Be renewed so that you can get to the next phase. If you skip the love phase, then the rest of your journey will be drudgery and you will be in danger of being a lawbreaker.

> *"Not everyone who says to Me, 'Lord, Lord,' shall enter the kingdom of heaven, but he who does the will of My Father in heaven. Many will say to Me in that day, 'Lord, Lord, have we not prophesied in Your name, cast out demons in Your name, and done many wonders in Your name?' And then I will declare to them, 'I never knew you; depart from Me, you who practice lawlessness!'"* (Matthew 7:21-23)

This is a strong statement, yet it comes from the mouth of our Lord Jesus Christ. Doing the works of the ministry for Him does not necessarily mean that you are doing His will, nor is it a proof of your love. Only those who do the will of the Father will enter the Kingdom of God. Could there be a higher will than doing the works of the ministry commanded by Jesus? When Jesus declared, *"I never knew you...you who practice lawlessness,"* it provides a shocking reality that

113

these works are not primarily what He is after. He wants to spend time with us.

If a husband, for example, never spends quality time with his precious wife but only provides for her, helps around the house, etc., he may let years go by and never truly get to know his wife. The wife appreciates all the work he does, but it is not fulfilling her. Eventually there will be a very definite communication problem. How much more we need constant communication with our Lord if we are to know Him and receive specific instructions on how to serve Him.

Love is what holds everything together. Love expressed in making time to know God is what He is after. Works done out of that relationship will be blessed and honored. The Youth With A Mission motto "To know God and to make Him known" clearly demonstrates the order in which things must go. If you are too busy to really spend that quality time with Him because you are doing His "will," then in effect you are actually out of His will. You have committed a grave error and have broken the law of love.

Though I speak with the tongues of men and of angels, but have not love...I am nothing. And though I bestow all my goods to feed the poor, and though I give my body to be burned, but have not love, it profits me nothing (1 Corinthians 13:1-3).

Sacrificing for God is of the utmost importance, yet it can still be done without love. Even if you choose to be a martyr and give up your life for His name's sake, you still can be operating in a spirit of religion and willpower and be greatly lacking in love. Terrorists willingly give up their lives for their god, yet does it prove that they have a true love relationship with God? Quite the contrary! The greatest sacrifice a person can give pales greatly in comparison to obedience to the law of love.

To do righteousness and justice [obedience] *is more acceptable to the Lord than sacrifice* (Proverbs 21:3).

In the same way, a husband may work hard for his wife's sake, yet never be able to say "I love you." He may try to justify himself by saying that his hard work and the fact that he provides for her proves his love. By doing this he feels that he is not required to mention the words "I love you." This is a false notion in our society today that we have carried with us into the Church and our relationship with Jesus. The Scriptures clearly point out the error and sin of this type of thinking. Doing evangelism and any other type of works without spending quality time with loving Him will result in a spirit of religion. It boils down to religion versus relationship. The religious person will evangelize by condemning and judging the sinner, while the person in love with Jesus will share that love and allow the Holy Spirit to convict others. Trying to help God in the convicting process always results in condemnation.

You will do the works of the ministry out of mercy or out of justice, depending on the love relationship you have with God. Love is one of those things that you can never discipline yourself to do. You can be disciplined to pray, read, work, etc., but never to love. You can only love if you spend time with God because God is love. Within yourself you cannot manufacture this fruit of the Spirit by mere works or discipline.

Owe no one anything expect to love one another, for he who loves another has fulfilled the law. For the commandments, "You shall not commit adultery," "You shall not murder," "You shall not steal," "You shall not bear false witness," "You shall not covet," and if there is any other commandment, are all summed up in this saying, namely, "You shall love your neighbor as yourself." Love does no harm to a neighbor; therefore love is the fulfillment of the law (Romans 13:8-10).

THE LOVELESS CHURCH

To the angel of the church of Ephesus write, "These things says He who holds the seven stars in His right hand, who walks in the midst of the seven golden lampstands: I know your works, your labor, your patience, and that you cannot bear those who are evil. And you have tested those who say they are apostles and are not, and have found them liars; and you have persevered and have patience, and have labored for My name's sake and have not become weary. **Nevertheless I have this against you, that you have left your first love.** *Remember therefore from where you have fallen; repent and do the first works, or else I will come to you quickly and remove your lampstand from its place— unless you repent'"*(Revelation 2:1-5).

The church of Ephesus is referred to as the loveless church. It seems hard to believe that they could be accused of being loveless with all their good works and sacrifices for the Lord. The problem is that the church of Ephesus made works a priority above their relationship with their Lord. They broke the law of love and thus were accused of a sin that would result in the church's light being taken from them.

God is sounding a warning to His people in these times. Churches and ministries that have been operating on this system of works and allowed their relationship with Jesus to drift will soon discover in this time of renewal that their lampstands will be taken from them. Influential ministries will lose their impact and be put on the shelf as a new breed of God-lovers will take their place. Churches once full will dwindle as the old wine runs dry as quickly as their first love did. If this has been the case for you or your church, you can change the situation. Return to your first love.

Nevertheless I have this against you, that you have left your first love. Remember therefore from where you have fallen; repent and do the first works... (Revelation 2:4-5).

If you are guilty of lovelessness then remember how it was when that love relationship was new, fresh, and exciting. Hours in His presence felt only like minutes. Return to that love you knew at first, your first love. Repent and tell Him that you want that relationship restored, and invite Him back to take first place in your life and ministry. These are the "first works" that verse 5 commands us to do. These works are not the great outward works of the ministry per se, but an inward work on our own hearts toward the Lord. To return to your first works is to return to your first Love. This is the cornerstone of every other work you will ever do. When you keep Him first you will not lose your reward.

He who has an ear, let him hear what the Spirit says to the churches. To him who overcomes I will give to eat from the tree of life, which is in the midst of the Paradise of God (Revelation 2:7).

What is the secret to this tree of life? The tree of life was found in the Garden of Eden. In that garden, before Adam and Eve sinned, there was perfect fellowship between God and man. They knew each other, talked together, and spent time together. The church of Ephesus, symbolic for us today, is exhorted to return to the original plan—perfect relationship with Him. That is where the tree of life can be found, in obedience to the law of love.

THE FATHER'S LOVE

The bride receives many blessings when she chooses to marry the groom. One of the most important benefits she has is to know his father's love. Before she chose to marry the groom, she had no access or relationship to the groom's father. Now that she is marrying the groom, the relationship is changed.

> *And in that day you will ask me nothing. Most assuredly, I say to you, whatever you ask the Father in My name He will give you. Until now you have asked nothing in My name. Ask, and you will receive, that your joy may be full* (John 16:23-24).

God the Father desires earnestly for us to have this relationship with Him. Most Christians deal only with Jesus but never go on to pursue a true relationship with their heavenly Father. This tragedy goes back to the Garden of Eden. The Father walked and talked in the Garden with Adam and Eve and they enjoyed a perfect relationship with Him—until sin came. At that time humankind became cut off from God and the relationship was broken.

You may be able to relate to this. Maybe you had a relationship with someone that was very close. Because of some offense or hurt your relationship with that person has been broken. You may often wish that this relationship would be restored, and the other person is probably thinking the same. But unless there is a humbling and step toward reconciliation on someone's part nothing may ever happen to restore your relationship. That is exactly how the Father feels toward us. He desperately wants to have His relationship restored with us, so He sent His only Son to die for us.

If we have accepted Jesus into our lives, and therefore married into the family of God, that relationship is restored on the Father's behalf. The problem is that even though this is true, most Christians can only relate to their heavenly Father as "Father" and not as "Daddy." Guilt and intimidation are still embedded into these precious Christians just as they came to Adam and Eve after they sinned. These believers still have the fear that if they get too close to the Father they may be found spiritually naked as Adam and Eve were in the Garden.

If this is a description of you, be encouraged. You are covered with the precious blood of Jesus. If you are in right relationship with Jesus, then God the Father sees Jesus when He sees you. He chooses to see you that way and not the way you see yourself. Don't let guilt and condemnation stop you from your relationship with your Father. He loves you so much and longs to have that close relationship with you.

And I have declared to them Your name, and will declare it, that the love with which You loved Me may be in them, and I in them (John 17:26).

If Adam and Eve never sinned in the first place but stayed in constant relationship with the Father, there would have been no need to send Jesus to die on the cross for our sins. We would already have eternal life. He sent Jesus to restore the relationship with the Father—not just so we would know Jesus, but so our relationship with the Father would be restored. That is how valuable the Father's relationship to you is. Eternal life was lost for man when sin came in. Knowing the Father in the Garden was the source of eternal life, and it still is the same today. Through Jesus Christ we can have eternal life because through Him we can have access to the Father. Jesus is our connection to the Father. Most people see Jesus as the end of the matter, but He is also the beginning of a new relationship in the Father's love, if we will allow it.

Eternal life is rooted in knowing the Father. Have you realized that throughout the centuries God's whole plan from Genesis to Revelation has been to restore His relationship with us? This is what eternal life is all about!

And this is eternal life, that they may know You, the only true God, and Jesus Christ whom You have sent (John 17:3).

Notice that this verse first mentions knowing God, referring to God as our Father, before the Son is mentioned. The Jews and the Muslims desperately want to have that Father's love. So they do many works and rituals in order to somehow try to please Him by fulfilling certain religious requirements. The Muslims for centuries have felt an inner hatred toward the Jews as they wanted to inherit the blessing from their common father, Abraham. As the story goes, Ishmael was the firstborn yet was rejected since he was conceived out of disobedience and works. Sarah and Abraham were trying to help God out (see Gen. 16).

Sarah propagated the plan to have Abraham conceive a son with one of their concubines. Basically, they did not trust God to bring about the promise. Since then, the Muslims have had a sense of rejection. They do even more rituals and works than the Jews in order to somehow attain the blessing of the Father's love. The Jews, by contrast, feel more confident of the fact that they were the ones chosen by God. Yet they still don't have a personal relationship with Him unless they have accepted Jesus as their long-awaited Messiah who will restore them back to a personal relationship with God the Father. Jews, Muslims, and the rest of the world need Jesus Christ in order to bring them into that relationship with the Father.

The present renewal is marked by a renewal of the Father's love. For many this has become a life-changing revelation. So many of us have trouble relating to God as our Daddy because maybe our earthly fathers did not know how to give or receive love. Earthly fathers sometimes turn out to be unemotional, rigid, critical, and unloving. Some of you have been abused by your fathers. If so, you probably have found it difficult to know and understand that your heavenly Daddy really loves you and wants to spend time with you.

He is never too busy for that. When the Father reveals His love you will be totally changed and receive a source of deep healing.

Ministers are also being changed by the Father's love and are thus able to express that love to their churches and through their ministries. In this way they are able to be the true father figures that they were called to be and become a source of healing to God's people.

Ask God to reveal this love to you if you have never experienced it and are craving for this love. This aspect of God's love is different from the love of Jesus and the Holy Spirit. To the degree that you will open yourself up to your Daddy without fear and condemnation, to that same degree you will be changed.

Prophetically, in this area of the renewal, the Father is asking His children to stop striving by their good works and ministries and simply receive His love. It is ours by His grace because of the price that His Son has already paid on the cross. Your heavenly Dad is waiting with open arms for you to come to Him just as you are.

CHAPTER 7

Questions and Concerns

So they were all amazed and perplexed, saying to one another, "Whatever could this mean?" Others mocking said, "They are full of new wine" (Acts 2:12-13).

As the master of the feast approaches Jesus, what kind of questions will he ask Him concerning the wedding? It is normal that questions will arise concerning the present move of God. If you have questions it shows that you probably mean business with God. I'd like to cover some common questions and reactions that may arise in the current renewal. Often due to fear—caused by a lack of knowledge and discernment—people miss out on what God is doing. Let's look at some of these questions and concerns you or others you know may be having.

"IT FRIGHTENS ME"

Some would say, "If the renewal is of God then it wouldn't frighten me!" Well, there are two types of fear.

For God has not given us a spirit of fear, but of power and of love and of a sound mind (2 Timothy 1:7).

The fear that satan brings robs us of faith and hope and makes us unable to love. This kind of fear is destructive.

On the other hand, there exists a godly fear that is the beginning of wisdom (see Prov. 9:10). Throughout the Bible, whenever God divinely visited His people, it produced fear. People are afraid of the unknown! Humankind does not fully know God, nor do we have Him figured out. Due to this, when our Holy God visits a mortal person in a more personal and powerful way, fear may arise.

When God shows up in ways we are already accustomed to, it often will not faze us. Eventually Christians can become too familiar with the normality of an overly organized and structured Christian life. God wants to shake and awake His people. If He has to surprise us to get our attention then He will do it. Our minds are too finite to understand the infinite ways of God. He is completely beyond us. When the sinfulness of man comes in contact with the holiness of God it can produce great fear—godly fear.

Suddenly a hand touched me, which made me tremble on my knees and on the palms of my hands. And he said to me, "O Daniel, man greatly beloved, understand the words that I speak to you, and stand upright, for I have now been sent to you." While he was speaking this word to me, I stood trembling. Then he said to me, "Do not fear, Daniel..." (Daniel 10:10-12).

This fear that Daniel had was not destructive but led to a great prayer victory revealing God's purposes for the endtimes. This fear also drew him closer to God with a reverence for how awesome He really is. Daniel did not allow this fear to hinder him from receiving from the Lord that which He had for him. Many people pray, "O Lord, visit your people today!" Then when He really does, they often don't want to believe that it's Him. It is too intense for them. A true visitation from God should produce the fruit of a more godly lifestyle and reverence for Him. Unfortunately, this is not always the case.

> *I was in the Spirit on the Lord's Day, and I heard behind me a loud voice, as of a trumpet…And when I saw Him, I fell at His feet as dead. But He laid His right hand on me, saying to me, "Do not be afraid; I am the First and the Last"* (Revelation 1:10,17).

Why would God have to continuously tell His people not to be afraid when He visited them? Evidently, it is because these men and women of God were really afraid! There is no hidden meaning here. It is plain that fear was involved. Now don't let fear draw you away from what He may want to reveal or bless you with. I am thankful that John did not allow fear to stop him from receiving the Book of Revelation, which informs us of end-time events and the fact that in the end, with Christ, we win! Godly fear is an instrument that God uses at times to grab our attention when He is serious about visiting us in a deeper way.

> *"Do you not fear Me?" says the Lord. "Will you not tremble at My presence…?"* (Jeremiah 5:22)

Another reason people may fear is because they begin to play games with the power of God. Ananias and Sapphira were in the middle of a great revival after Pentecost. In its infancy the move was in danger due to sin from within the camp. They lied to the Holy

Spirit. What was God's response in order to insure the protection of that renewal and revival?

> *Then Ananias, hearing these words, fell down and breathed his last.* **So great FEAR came upon all those who heard these things** (Acts 5:5).

I heard a true story that happened in 1994. The new wine of the Holy Spirit had begun to come upon a certain church. The pastor and the congregation were being renewed. Two elders were totally against what was happening, partly because they did not understand it all, and so they made up their minds that it was not of God. They immediately set out to stop the move however they could. The final result for these two men was that one died in a car accident, and the other died for an unknown reason the same night. Godly fear came upon the church, and the renewal continued with even greater power similar to the book of Acts Annanias and Saphira account.

Fear can be turned into a blessing if it comes from God for His purposes. If you have fear, let it draw you closer to Him. If it is a fear from the devil, resist it and take authority over it in the name of Jesus. The love that God has for us will vanquish all ungodly fear.

"It May Cause Division"

Division is a common concern, especially among pastors and leaders who are responsible for their congregations. Some think that if this renewal is of God it should not cause any division, but there are different types of division. Division in some cases can be a blessing. Most of the greatest moves of God caused a division somewhere.

When Luther discovered the revolutionary truth that salvation comes by faith and not by works, he was separated from the established Church of his day. That new move of God caused a great

126

division, and yet it rediscovered the greatest hidden truth about salvation. When the Great Awakening broke out in New Jersey in the year 1725, it was also violently opposed by the more traditional churches.

Those involved in a previous move of God often become the persecutors of the present move if they are not careful. We must learn from history lest we commit the same error and unconsciously find ourselves fighting against God.

In the early Church there was division among the believing Jews at the thought that Gentiles could also inherit salvation. We can be grateful to God for the division that allowed the salvation message to spread to the nations. Jesus Christ caused division almost everywhere He went. Jesus is the Prince of Peace to those who follow Him in Spirit and in truth. On the same note, Jesus also mentioned that *"a man's enemies will be those of his own household"* (Matt. 10:36).

It is within the church that God decides to move among His people. Some people will gladly go with the flow of what God is doing. Unfortunately, there will be those who will not, and they may leave or cause havoc in the church. The fruit of backbiting, slander, rebellion, and hatred are worldly and will cause the Kingdom of God to be divided in a destructive way. Those who engage in these "bad fruits" and stay in the church can quench the move of God. That is why God in His mercy will allow some churches to lose certain members for a season in order to protect the church and keep it from self-destruction.

After this kind of division, a church becomes more solid in the unity of the Spirit. God will multiply the church that is on a more solid foundation. Of course, it is not easy to watch angry brothers and sisters in the Lord leave with bitterness because they cannot accept what God is doing. But the church has become like someone who has a cancer: when the doctor cuts out the disease, it may hurt, but it will save that person's life in the long run. We need to keep our eyes fixed on the long run, instead of the temporal, in order to save the life of the Church at large. Don't quench this move of God out of a fear of man just because a few people may be against it. Pray for them and love them, but obey God rather than man.

God is restructuring His Church so that it will be flexible enough to handle His glory and the influx of millions of new converts into the Kingdom of God! He will first purify and cleanse His people, cutting out the infection and healing the wounds to preserve the life of the church so that it can handle new wine. God's division is actually only temporary and will eventually promote true unity and health. Division that comes from satan, if left undealt with, will promote destruction.

God wants to pour new wine into new wineskins. Some Christians and churches need to become new wineskins in order to be able to handle the new wine of the Spirit and not collapse under its potency. We must decide if we are willing to pay the price for renewal and revival in our lives and churches. We cannot allow ungodly fear to enter in. God will bless what comes from Him. It's during the transition time of this new move of God that we need to hold on tight to the Holy Spirit and trust Him to take us through to major revival and bring in the harvest.

"It's Too Emotional"

Christians sometimes have the notion that if there is too much emotion, then it must not be of God. The Bible also has much to say on this subject. King David danced for joy in the presence of the Lord. He was so caught up in the Lord that he became extremely emotional and he danced before the Lord naked. This, of course, bothered his wife (see 2 Sam. 6). (I am not advocating that anyone tries this.)

Jesus was so full of emotion that He angrily stormed into the temple courts and overthrew the tables of the moneychangers. Not only that, His anger led Him to go one step further and make a whip that He used to chase out the moneychangers (see John 2:13-15).

When the World Cup of soccer is playing and the favored team has just scored, you don't have to search far to find millions of people around the world—including Christians—gathered together with great emotion. Why? They have just had the revelation that their favorite team may win the game. Yelling, jumping up and down, laughing, and even crying can follow. If this is the case in every nation when it comes to sports, then why is it such a big problem when God's people come in contact with the living God and become emotional? We often treat our God-given emotions like a disease.

I am not advocating emotionalism, but when a person is emotional *because* the Spirit of the living God has touched his or her soul, it is a natural response. We should not criticize it. Even if we suspect that a person may be faking it, we should not overreact unless we know what they are doing is truly ungodly. In these situations, the gift of discernment will be there to guide us.

Jonathan Edwards said, "Nothing of religious significance ever took place in the human spirit if it wasn't deeply affected by such godly emotions."[1] In this renewal I have often noticed that many of the people who are overcome with outbursts of laughter or crying are people who are not normally emotional and who have rarely been able to express such emotions in years. God knows the heart of each person and his or her inner needs. Often, just a simple word from the Lord of some past hurt that God is healing will open up the emotional realm that has been blocked by that hurt. In many cases this unhealed hurt has affected the personality of the person.

Like I mentioned several times, you should not be *led* by emotions. But if you are truly being visited by the Holy Spirit, then do not be afraid if the Holy Spirit chooses to *touch* your emotions. It may very well be a source of healing in your life.

John White said, "The lack of emotion is just as sick as being controlled by emotions."[2] For some people the fear of being the center of attention may be the root of the fear of expressing emotion. Is it always wrong if attention is being drawn toward a person? It really depends. I can't help but notice someone who is overcome by the Spirit of God. Often God will use someone who will not necessarily speak a message with their mouth, but they will become the message themselves.

In Ezekiel 4:4, Ezekiel is commanded by God to lie on his side for 430 days (symbolic of the 430 years of Israel's disobedience) and then later on to shave his head and beard to show the future of the city at the time. He definitely became the center of attention, but it was in order to give attention to what God wanted to communicate through him. Ezekiel became the message. The prostitute who washed Jesus' feet with her tears also became the message (see Luke 7:37-38). Saul, as we mentioned earlier, became the message when he came into the proximity of the prophets and prophesied naked (see 1 Sam. 19). He became a message to himself of humility forced by God.

"SOME GET INTO THE FLESH"

Sometimes people get the notion that in a time of great outpouring God uses only perfect people who are always in the Spirit. I once heard a fellow Bible school student accuse another student of "dancing in the flesh" and not in the Spirit during a time of corporate worship. He replied, "Of course I'm in the flesh, and so are you. If we were both out of the flesh we would be dead by now!" There is some truth to this. Until we are in Heaven we will always see people acting in the flesh in one way or another, no matter how anointed they are. Paul and Barnabas even had a heated discussion about whether or not they were going to take John Mark with them on their second missionary journey (see Acts 15:37-39). The Kingdom of God advanced despite some division and carnality on their part.

You can't pinpoint one case of carnality and human error and conclude then that the whole move must be in error. One of the great revivalists prayed to God for a perfect revival. He then said that if he must settle for an imperfect revival he would still take revival no matter how it comes.

Now I, John, saw and heard these things. And when I heard and saw, I fell down to worship before the feet of the angel who showed me these things. Then he said to me, "See that you do not do that…" (Revelation 22:8-9).

John was tempted to worship the angel—which would have been carnality and sin. How could John have been so much in the flesh after such an encounter? This passage clearly warns of the carnality of idolatry. Idolizing certain truths or messengers of Good News instead of Jesus Himself has always been a problem. And it will be a great problem in the last days, as the Scriptures imply here. Yet this error did not discontinue or discredit the revelation he received.

The reason John was preserved from this error was because he heeded the angel's rebuke. John Wesley also had bitter disputes with other godly men over doctrinal issues, as did Martin Luther. The fact that men and women of God will have the tendency to revert to operating in the flesh at times does not necessarily negate the genuineness of their ministry or an entire move of God.

Peter acted in the flesh probably more than the other apostles. He even tried to stop Jesus from going to the cross, which was the world's only hope of salvation. Peter continued by cutting off the servant's ear only hours later when the guards came to get Jesus. Then, he denied ever knowing the Lord after swearing to Jesus that he would never deny Him. As if this was not enough, he even reverted back to the law of the Jews by not eating with Gentiles. This was after he already had a vision signifying that he should not regard certain foods or fellowshiping with other Gentile believers as unholy. Then at other times when the religious Jews were not around, Peter would eat again with the Gentile believers. This hypocrisy caused Paul's anger to flare. (See Matthew 16:22; 26:33-35, 51,69-75; Acts 10; Galatians 2:11-14.)

These cases of carnality and sin were all covered by the blood of Jesus through repentance. God is always willing to forgive when we repent. Repentance is the key attitude. A teachable and repentant heart will always protect you from the downfall of the flesh. If the Lord rebukes someone and he or she truly repents, it is the end of the discussion. Satan is the culprit who tempts our flesh which is constantly at war with our spirit. He wants to discredit what God is doing by exposing our tendency to revert to operating in the carnal realm. Praise be to Jesus, for the blood that He shed can deliver us and provide a way to overcome and protect us from our fleshly nature.

MOTIVES

I would like to end this chapter by again emphasizing that it is not wrong to have questions about what is happening in this renewal, but we need to be honest about what the motives are behind our questions. If your questions are for the purpose of finding out more about the Holy Spirit and the way He is moving, that's fine. To be a "noble Berean" is a good trait (see Acts 17:10-11 KJV). I encourage you to search for the truth diligently with prayer until you find it and are at peace. Once you find it though, press in and receive it!

If you think what is happening is against your personality, then don't let your personality hinder you from receiving from the Holy Spirit during this season of divine visitation. Maybe you are afraid. Seek God and find out why. His sheep hear His voice. Once you are convinced this move is of God, don't run from Him and His presence. He is a loving Father and only wants the best for His children. He loves you!

If you are purposely trying to hinder others from receiving more of this renewal—and, thus, more of God—because you are not certain it is from God, then you may very well be treading on some very dangerous ground. If this is the case, I counsel you to take Gamaliel's advice.

> *And now I say to you, keep away from these men and let them alone; for if this plan or this work is of men, it will come to nothing; but if it is of God, you cannot overthrow it—lest you even be found to fight against God (Acts 5:38-39).*

Don't make the mistake of judging this move until you have thoroughly seen it, experienced it, and have seen the fruit that it brings into people's lives. Search your heart and walk in the wisdom of the Lord. There is great blessing and anointing ahead for you if you can allow the new wine to transform you from the inside out.

ENDNOTES

1. Jonathan Edwards, *A Treatise Concerning Religious Affection* (Cosimo Classics, June 1, 2007, http://www.cosimobooks.com/b1157_A-Treatise-Concerning-Religious-Affections-1602065454-9781602065451.htm).

2. John White, *When the Spirit Comes with Power* (InterVarsity Press, June 1988).

CHAPTER 8

New Wine Anointings

And he said to him, "Every man at the beginning sets
out the good wine, and when the guests have well drunk,
then the inferior. You have kept the good wine until now!"
(John 2:10)

The guests who will benefit the most from the new wine are those who will stay until the end. The best is yet to come. This is especially true for those who will linger around until the end drinking in the new wine, instead of only tasting the wine and leaving.

This outpouring of the Holy Spirit is not just a matter of uncontrollable laughter and joy. This is only the beginning of a greater visitation of God. Yes, God is healing and restoring His people. But one thing is for sure: it does not stop there. The next phase is even more intense. God wants to empower us with new anointings once we have been renewed—anointings with much more voltage than in previous moves. Those who are experiencing these new anointings are seeing dramatic differences in their lives and ministries. The ones getting empowered in such a way are those who are continuously crying out, "More, Lord!"

If you know that you already have an anointing on your life, then I challenge you to go further in this process of renewal, allowing yourself to be emptied and refilled. An even greater anointing than you have ever known before is what is in store for your life! It is a "fresh" anointing. God is changing the oil in our lamps and putting in fresh oil. This is part of the worldwide renewal of the Body of Christ. As this process of renewal reaches its climax, it will overflow into the greatest worldwide revival that the Church has ever seen! This is the reason God is dispersing incredible anointings upon His people for revival.

In January of 1994 many different churches in different countries began to experience an incredible outpouring of the Holy Spirit. It was much more widespread than even that of the Azusa Street Revival, and it has not stopped since. To this day thousands of new ministries have been birthed that have reached millions of people around the world. Not only have other multiple moves of God resulted but a great harvest of souls around the world has exploded as so many more people are doing crusades, street evangelism, planting churches, and now many are starting to infiltrate industries other "mountains" like Hollywood and media, the business arena, false religions, politics, and so much more. Each wave of renewal, leading to a revival of God's people, ultimately leads to a harvest of souls. Revival begins in your heart right now, it is not necessarily an event or place but a state of being.

What could this mean? Why did a similar visitation of the Holy Spirit occur around the same time internationally? Could it be that

God is no longer interested in using only one nation or church to spread revival? Could he be setting the stage for the greatest revival ever recorded before the return of our Lord Jesus Christ, as prophesied in the Bible? You decide!

FILLED TO THE BRIM

Several months after we were first touched by this new anointing and renewal in Jerusalem, we were scheduled to minister in a church in Fort Myers, Florida. I began to ask God to pour upon our lives an even greater anointing than we had ever known. Certainly we had already experienced incredible personal revival, and we noticed that the anointing we had received increased while we ministered. Yet I sensed that there was an even greater wave of God's power awaiting us. I could not just fly over to some renewal hot spot to get it this time. There was no time. We had a flight to Europe scheduled within days. I trusted that God would meet me where I was at and touch me again.

The next day, my wife and I were in a store at a shopping mall where we met a Christian woman. When we asked her if she had experienced renewal, she not only told us she had, but that she had also recognized us from some renewal meetings in Canada. Apparently, we had attended the same meetings. She invited us to her local church that night to share in their prayer meeting. When we arrived a small number of people were praying throughout the building. We immediately sensed the same anointing of renewal in that church as we had been experiencing. We shared our experiences with the group. Then we asked the pastor to pray over us to receive another wave of renewal and power.

Up to this point, I had not manifested in any unusual way. When I had ministered, others had begun to receive renewal with certain manifestations that had occurred as a result of God's power.

This night, it was my turn to receive not only a manifestation but a greater anointing. I never was one who got into emotionalism, but I was willing to let God have His way with me, whatever the outcome would be.

As they began to pray, an incredible surge of power consumed my entire being! I fell to the floor and began to shake violently. It was really like being plugged into a very powerful electric current. I must have been shaking like this for over an hour. I'm sure it was quite a scene to behold. I felt totally given over to the Holy Spirit with no resistance. I surely did not fully understand what was happening until later. One thing I did know, I was receiving an anointing stronger than I had ever known. I could barely handle it, but it was so good. I kept crying out to God for even more because I did not want to have this opportunity pass me by until I got all that God had for me that night. I truly did not want to miss a thing.

I wanted to receive as much as God would give me to impact as many people as possible with this anointing. My wife also received a new and increased anointing. While she was standing up her body became very hot—so hot that she almost could not handle it anymore. The pastor laughed and told her to give some of this fire to me. As I was on the floor, still trembling, she laid her burning hands on me. I thought to myself, *How much more of this can I take?* At that moment the fire of God came all over me. During this time I began to have an even deeper burden for lost souls who are on their way to hell without a personal relationship with Jesus Christ. I wept profusely for their salvation.

On that special day we were reempowered for more effective ministry. I discovered that the anointing as an evangelist was much greater and easier to flow in. I felt an added boldness and a sharper discernment than I had known before. Other gifts of the Spirit were also accentuated. I began to prophesy with a greater freedom and accuracy. We saw many more healings take place either through word of knowledge or when our hands would start to burn with the same intense heat. Deliverance over people who were extremely bound took much less time as the newer anointing seemed to carry with it a greater authority and discernment against demonic activity.

We realized that the anointing had increased and we flowed in certain gifts with much more power and assurance than we had previously. For instance, Stephanie began prophesying with a more powerful and precise gift of prophecy. She also received prophetic dreams much more frequently. Prior to this, I would never prophesy publicly over a person but would leave that to the prophets. The spirit of prophecy began to come on me and the Holy Spirit began to ask me to do these things more frequently. Most importantly, our personal relationship with Jesus became more and more intimate as we were often filled with a new joy. I do not want to sound like I am boasting as I write these things. They are simply precious experiences that I want to share with you so that you too will have a hunger to receive more of Him and more of this anointing for yourself.

Two days after that experience in Florida, we were scheduled to preach at three services on a Sunday. Each service seemed to explode with much power and many outward signs: laughing, screaming, falling, crying, physical healings, miracles. By the time the evening service arrived, the anointing had multiplied and so had the faith of the people. They invited their backslidden friends and family, and many came back to a personal relationship with Jesus. It was beautiful to see families in tears as they were reunited (though the church did get noisy with all the things God was doing). It was a very blessed series of meetings.

The next day we departed for France. When we arrived we attended a pastors' meeting in Paris with about 15 pastors. We were asked to share about the renewal. They wanted to know what all the commotion was about concerning the recent move of the Holy Spirit in North America and parts of Europe. We testified to these pastors about our experiences, and we told them that the fresh out-pouring of the Holy Spirit is not just for a special church or city, but for anyone hungry enough to receive it. A pastor who had just returned from England testified about the same renewal sweeping the whole country. A third pastor then shared that the same renewal started in January of 1994 in a small church in a town in the south of France. Renewal had started in their church after they had fasted and prayed for ten days, yet they were unaware that it was happening anywhere else!

These pastors began to explode saying, "We're jealous. Give us what you have received!" We prayed for them and many of them wept on their faces on the hard floor. Others laughed hysterically as they were filled with a new joy. These European pastors and missionaries began to see their congregations touched by this wave of renewal and joy in countries that had been spiritually dry for years. Since that time we have seen many more churches, Christian leaders and pastors in Europe and the United States renewed, refilled, and empowered with a new anointing and joy for the greatest of revivals to come. Let us now take a closer look at these new anointings!

WHO CAN BE ANOINTED?

And it shall come to pass afterward that I will pour out My Spirit on all flesh; your sons and your daughters shall prophesy, your old men shall dream dreams, your young men shall see visions. And also on My menservants and on My maidservants I will pour out My Spirit in those days (Joel 2:28-29).

As we see clearly in these passages, God is able to pour out His Spirit on anyone who will receive it. Young and old, rich and poor, male and female. I've seen little children pray for the sick and prophesy and evangelize with incredible boldness, convicting even adults to be saved. We have been blessed as elderly and retired believers have often backed us up in some of the most powerful intercessory prayer. The anointing for service is for any believer. It is not reserved only for those recognized as ministers. The anointing goes beyond the five-fold ministry gifts of apostle, prophet, evangelist, pastor, or teacher.

In one meeting a young man walked into the service on his way to a local bar to get drunk with his friend. He decided to walk into the service for the fun of it, as he thought he would get a good laugh. He insincerely asked people to pray for him. As they did the Holy Spirit came upon this unsaved young man and knocked him to the floor. He turned white with fear! He realized at that moment that this was no joke. He had come in contact with a living God who would not be mocked—and who meant business with his soul. The person praying then asked him if he would like to accept Jesus into his life. He responded by almost begging, "Please tell me how I can be saved!" He was in a hurry to make his peace with God that night.

The next night the young man came again with some of his unsaved friends and they also received salvation. The newly converted young man prayed over his friends with the same anointing that the church's ministry team was ministering under. People were falling to the floor and some received a mighty deliverance. Within a 24-hour period the young man who thought it was all a joke was saved, delivered, evangelizing, and flowing in the same anointing as the other ministers. He was permitted to pray for his friends while some of the ministry team monitored him to make sure everything went well. This is an example of how God can anoint whom He wants when He wants. His ways are higher than our ways.

*And also on My menservants and My maidservants I will pour
out My Spirit in those days* (Joel 2:29).

A definition of a *manservant* in this text is a "slave." In the Old
Testament a slave would never be permitted to perform any priestly
or ministerial function in the temple. It was reserved only for the
priests who were consecrated for this kind of service. In Acts 2:16-21
Peter preached this same passage in Joel, declaring that this
prophecy was now being fulfilled and the Spirit was for any believer
to be used in His service. Finally, the time had come that not only a
priest or minister could be used of God. This anointing can be given
to any believer for ministry in as much power as anyone else.

Philip was not an apostle, but one who served tables—a waiter!
He became so full of the anointing that he was about to burst. He
departed, led by the Holy Spirit, to Samaria and preached Christ
with signs and wonders following. Many conversions took place and
the whole city was rejoicing (see Acts 8). In fact, when the believers
were scattered after Pentecost, the ordinary believers went out
wherever they were scattered and spread the Gospel, while the apostles stayed back in Jerusalem (see Acts 8:1).

Those who were scattered everywhere preaching the gospel
were teenagers, mothers, working men, the elderly, etc. It is not just
a privilege but it is the trademark of a true believer to do the works
of Jesus with such an anointing. In fact, if believers are not doing
some of these things some of the time in some way, then there is a
problem somewhere.

*And these signs will follow those who believe: In My name they
will cast out demons; they will speak with new tongues; they will
take up serpents; and if they drink anything deadly, it will by no
means hurt them; then they will lay hands on the sick, and they
will recover* (Mark 16:17-18).

If you are a believer, you qualify! This passage does not say that only pastors and evangelists would do these things. It plainly says any believer will, and has the ability to, accomplish these things. Are you a believer in Jesus Christ? Then rejoice because you are never unemployed in God's Kingdom. God is pouring out His Spirit in such a way because He wants to use all of us. He cannot finish the task ahead only with those already in the "ministry."

God is preparing an all-out attack against the kingdom of darkness to snatch away millions of souls from destruction and into His Kingdom! He longs to anoint you for greater service, no matter what your present circumstance or position in life may be. Jesus Himself said that you would do greater works than He did! (see John 14:12). Don't be surprised at the fresh anointing coming upon the Church for this purpose. The anointing is extra powerful because He wants to get the job done right and in less time because the days are short as we near the end of an age. Be ready to say, "Here I am, Lord, use me!"

PROPHETIC ANOINTINGS

In the Old Testament, no manservant or maidservant (or slaves) is ever mentioned even once as functioning as a prophet. At Pentecost God changed this so that believers in every strata of society could be used to prophesy as the Spirit came upon them. Whenever the Holy Spirit has moved in a fresh way throughout the history of the Church, it has often been accompanied by prophecy. There has been a significant increase in the prophetic anointing in this renewal. It comes upon whomever God chooses, and whoever is hearing what the Spirit is saying.

A person with the ministry gift of the prophet may not always be around in the church when God may want to speak. More and more people are obeying the call of God on their lives to be prophets, but God will not be limited if one is not around or may not realize his or her calling. God will use anybody He chooses for the moment. Even if there is a prophet present, it still does not disqualify others from ministering prophetically.

In each of our meetings we need to come with an expectancy that God is going to speak to His people. We need to be sensitive to the Holy Spirit and to the fact that He may want to use us in the area of prophecy. The spirit of prophecy can also be contagious. Look at what happened to Saul in the Book of Samuel:

> *When they came there to the hill, there was a group of prophets to meet him; then the Spirit of God came upon him, and he prophesied among them. And it happened, when all who knew him formerly saw that he indeed prophesied among the prophets, that the people said to one another, "What is this that has come upon the son of Kish? Is Saul also among the prophets?"* (1 Samuel 10:10-11)

Saul happened to be just a little too close to the prophets. The spirit of prophecy upon the prophets overtook him. You too can flow more easily in this gift when there are several others flowing very strongly in this gift around you. In those moments you must simply speak out what God gives you. He will give you more as you continue in it. Like any gift, prophecy is performed by faith. Again, let me emphasize that just because God uses you to prophesy does not mean that you are a prophet! You are simply flowing with the spirit of prophecy for that moment in time.

The gifts of prophecy flow hand in hand with worship and music. First Samuel 10:5 lists several instruments that were to accompany the prophets, consisting of stringed instruments, tambourine, flute, and harp, which are also symbols of instruments in general. When the Holy Spirit asks me to prophesy I will often look for a guitar or keyboard player to accompany me, and then I begin worshiping to set the atmosphere for prophecy. It flows much better that way. Sometimes the instruments alone can be played as a prophetic expression to the Lord. This can be compared to someone who gives a message in tongues while someone else interprets. It is a matter of flowing with the Holy Spirit. The key is to be obedient to His voice.

At times my wife will start trembling when God is giving her a prophetic message. How the message is communicated may differ with each person. God may ask you to do something contrary to your natural way of doing things. Just obey and leave the results to God. The spirit of prophecy can be released in different ways, just as it was in the Book of Acts:

And as we stayed many days, a certain prophet named Agabus came down from Judea. When he had come to us, he took Paul's belt, bound his own hands and feet, and said, "Thus says the Holy Spirit, So shall the Jews at Jerusalem bind the man who owns this belt, and deliver him into the hands of the Gentiles" (Acts 21:10-11).

The Holy Spirit may direct you to act out the message that He gives you by using the material things that surround you. When the person receiving the prophecy can see something tangible correlating to the prophecy, it increases his or her faith. Never limit the spirit of prophecy. Just let it flow through you and the Holy Spirit will guide you as to what to do.

If you are a member of a local church who has never been known to prophesy and you have a prophecy to give, you should first go to your pastor or the minister in charge of the meeting. Tell him (or her) that you have a word and what it is as far as you know. As the shepherd called to train the flock, the pastor or leader is responsible for what happens, to a large degree, in a church service. We need to submit to one another with the gifts. If the pastor or minister tells you not to prophesy or to save it for another meeting where he feels the word would be more appropriate, just go with it. This way your job is done. The pastor is now accountable to God to allow the prophetic word to go forth, if he judges it right to do so.

Eventually, people will recognize those truly flowing with the gift of prophecy and those who are not. If your prophetic utterances are consistently accurate, you will gain trust from the leadership to speak what God gives you and may even be trusted to prophesy more regularly. If most of the time your prophecies are totally off, then you need to check the problem out with God. To monitor this for those who are just starting to prophesy, it is a good idea for the minister in charge to ask the person who just received the prophecy if it was accurate.

These guidelines eliminate disorder in the church and leave room for those who are learning from God and developing this gift. Those whose prophecies are way off are not to be automatically labeled as false prophets. It just may be that they need to be more sensitive to the Holy Spirit. If all this encouraging and correction is done in a spirit of love, it will encourage the congregation to flow in the gifts without fear of failure. We need to leave room for learning even if that means making a few mistakes.

As I mentioned earlier, the spirit of prophecy can be contagious, so there must be some order. If 20 people start to prophesy with no one to monitor them, it can take up the whole service. Remember that the spirit of prophecy is subject to the prophets (see 1 Cor. 14:32). If you are asked to hold your prophecy for the Wednesday night service, don't be alarmed. Your prophecy won't vanish into thin air. God is more than able to give you the word again in another meeting. It's one thing to receive a message, yet it is another thing to know when to give it. We don't always know it all, and that is why we need to be submitted one to another without getting offended.

> *Pursue love, and desire spiritual gifts, but especially that you may prophesy....But he who prophesies speaks edification and exhortation and comfort to men. He who speaks in a tongue edifies himself, but he who prophesies edifies the church* (1 Corinthians 14:1,3-4).

Another manner in which God communicates prophecy to us is through visions and dreams. Acts 2:17 mentions that old men shall dream dreams and young men shall see visions when the Holy Spirit is being poured out. Often while praying for a meeting that I'm scheduled to minister in, I will see in the Spirit what will happen during that service. It will often turn out exactly as God has revealed it to me. This helps me to pray in a more precise manner in conjunction with what God is revealing to me for that particular service. My wife will often have dreams about situations that will arise or dangers that can be avoided if we will pray. These days we pay much more attention to dreams as they have been a source of protection and direction during very crucial times in our ministry.

Don't discard your dreams or visions. Write them down and pray about them. Often God can communicate to our human spirit much more easily while our mind, will, and emotions are at rest, thus making it easier for us to receive from God. God is pouring out the spirit of prophecy in a greater measure in this renewal. When you are renewed, full of the anointing, and spending more time in His presence, you will be much more able to receive prophetic revelation than when you are not abiding in Him.

If you think you have a prophetic word, dream, or vision for someone, once you have prayed over it, by all means tell that person.

Your obedience in those crucial times may even save someone from tragedy or make a difference between life and death in some cases. It is much better to step out in faith and possibly fail than to hold back and cause someone to miss out on what God has for him or her.

As I minister in the prophetic according to the Lord's leading, the Lord will have me combine the gifts of words of knowledge and prophecy. For instance, I had a word of knowledge about a man's past that was coupled with a word of prophecy. So I spoke about what God was going to do in his life in the future if he would allow the Lord to restore him. Later he shared with me that the word that I had spoken was a confirmation. God had told him the exact same thing the day before as he was meditating on the Scriptures.

God wants to pour out upon us this gift of prophecy in stronger doses than in previous times to prepare His people now for what lies ahead in the very near future. What we know now is only a foretaste of what is being prepared for this generation. We are only getting our feet wet; soon we will be swimming in the fast-moving current of revival.

INTERCESSORS

God is raising up intercessors who will stand in the gap to see mighty prayer victories and to ultimately pray in a mighty harvest of lost souls. When the new wine of the Holy Spirit comes upon some, they will begin to weep and travail as never before. The Holy Spirit wants to intercede through His people. After you receive a new anointing you may be one to whom God will give this special task. Often intercessors will even be awakened in the night to intercede in prayer for different circumstances. In my opinion, intercession is one of the highest calls upon a person's life. An intercessor actually works alongside our Lord Jesus in a most special and intimate way. The reason for this is that Jesus has been seated in Heaven in His present role as Intercessor ever since He joined the Father after His resurrection. He continually intercedes for His children and the world.

During this renewal many more intercessors are now joining the ranks in this most strategic ministry. When the spirit of intercession comes upon a person he or she is able to pray with unusual boldness and the assurance that breaks the chains of darkness and ushers in great victories. Hours can go by but may seem only like minutes. As with prophecy, the spirit of intercession can, does, and will come upon any believer as He chooses, though some are called to intercession as a full-time ministry.

We all need to ask the Holy Spirit to pray through us and be sensitive to Him when He does. However, we should not always expect a spirit of intercession when we are having our regular prayer time. It is much easier to pray when the spirit of intercession comes, though we must never cease praying. We are still to continuously pray in faith, even when we don't feel that anything is happening.

Some of the greatest revivals and moves of God in churches and nations have happened not so much because of the evangelists, but because of the faithful intercessors who were in the background. Most of these intercessors were not recognized here on this earth, but their reward will be the greatest in Heaven. It appears that many more women than men are engaged in deep intercession as a full-time ministry. I believe that God has called many more men to this type of ministry but many have yet to be obedient to the Holy Spirit's call. I can say that faithful intercessors around the world are the backbone that undergirds our ministry.

When we go somewhere to minister we always make it our aim to be thoroughly covered by intercessory prayer before, during, and even after an outreach or meeting. Since we started doing this several years ago we have seen practically a 100 percent increase in souls saved, healings, miracles, etc. On numerous occasions we have been saved from near-death accidents due to this prayer backup.

The difference between having consistent intercession for any ministry or not having it is phenomenal. Reinhard Bonnke, the German evangelist who has seen over 1,600,000 people in attendance in a single crusade in Africa, has over 500 full-time intercessors. He also has several full-time intercessory coordinators. Besides this, many thousands of Christians support him worldwide and also cover his meetings in prayer. In his ministry, consistent prayer is organized months before, during, and after the crusades are finished. His ministry recruits intercessors from within the churches of those countries that participate and sponsor the crusade meetings. No wonder his ministry has seen hundreds of thousands of people accept Christ in a single service with great signs and wonders! He personally attributes the success of his ministry to his faithful intercessors.

God is pouring out the Spirit of intercession upon His people because worldwide revival is on His agenda. Ministers and intercessors are working together more and more in this way. One may be the mouthpiece that reaps while the other is battling the powers of darkness making way for the Spirit of God to come through. Both are extremely important. We must realize the hidden power of intercession. Ministers often forget to utilize it, which often leaves them wondering why their good preaching did not get the job done.

Pastor Yonggi Cho pastors a church of over 830,000 people (as of 2007) in Seoul, Korea. Cho's ministry places the highest importance on prayer; he attributes prayer with the church's success. When asked what his secret was to building the largest church in the world he replied very simply, "I pray and I obey."

Imagine how much more God can do through us as He is pouring out His Spirit in a fresh way and dispersing a greater anointing for intercession upon His children. The greatest victories are yet to be won on our knees!

When Israel was fighting against the Amelekites, Moses had the authority to win the battle just by keeping his hands lifted up. The problem was that his hands grew weary. Many Christian leaders have the authority to win but lack intercessors who will hold up their hands when the battles of life and ministry rage. When they lack intercessors in these crucial times they can be in great danger.

> *And so it was, when Moses held up his hand, that Israel prevailed; and when he let down his hand, Amalek prevailed. But Moses' hands became heavy; so they took a stone and put it under him, and he sat on it. And Aaron and Hur supported his hands, one on one side, and the other on the other side; and his hands were steady until the going down of the sun. So Joshua defeated Amalek and his people with the edge of the sword* (Exodus 17:11-13).

You may very well be the one to hold up the hands of a weary Moses (your pastor for starters) to see these battles won. Will you take up the burden to intercede even if you are not noticed except by your Savior Jesus Christ?

REVELATION IN THE WORD

The Holy Spirit is revealing certain truths found in the Word of God. Those under this anointing of revelation can open the Bible and discover deep revelations directly from the Holy Spirit. It seems that profound truths just flow when this anointing is at work. This anointing is very important, especially for those who teach or minister the Word of God in some way. God is equipping His people with His Word in ways that bypass traditional and religious concepts of analyzing the Scriptures. He wants His people trained on how to use the Sword of the Spirit, which is the Word of God, to cut through the thoughts and motives of the heart of man (see Eph. 6:17; Heb. 4:12).

The gift of revelation through the Word of God is an amazing gift. It can revolutionize a whole move of God and help keep God's people from ignorance. When Martin Luther rediscovered the "hidden" truth that salvation is by faith, it changed the history of the Church. That particular revelation was manifested through this anointing. One verse that becomes revelation can make a profound impact in many lives. Those who are enlightened by a certain revelation will then pass it on to others. God's holy Word is always there for us to read and meditate on, yet when this anointing comes it makes the Word come alive and speak directly to our hearts. There are still many truths in the Word of God at our disposal that we are not applying. These truths are still waiting to be rediscovered, and when they are, they could cause another reformation!

When the Holy Spirit fell at Pentecost, Peter began to have the gift of revelation quickened to him from Joel 2:28, *"And it shall come to pass afterward...."* The Word of God in the Book of Joel was always there for the religious Jews to read. But they could not fully understand or apply this truth until it was revealed through the anointing of revelation upon Peter. Many teachers and authors move in this gift of revelation through the Word. Yet we need to see many more ministers and Christians alike empowered with this gift to keep the present renewal in accordance with the Word of God.

This revelation from the Word is often explained as a *rhema* word: a "now" word that can be applied specifically to a person's life and circumstance. A *logos* word is a Scripture or passage any

Christian can read in the Word without it necessarily becoming a personal revelation.

If the Holy Spirit begins to drop a revelation upon you from the Word of God, it is best to immediately write it down somewhere and study it. If you don't, the anointing may lift and you may forget what the revelation was. We should be zealous to have this anointing come upon us if the Holy Spirit so chooses. We should eagerly desire all the spiritual gifts and then use them to edify each other as First Corinthians 14 commands us to do. When you receive this kind of revelation from Heaven you will find it a great, exciting privilege. It will also be like manna from Heaven for those in a time of spiritual famine with whom you share your revelation.

The Preacher sought to find acceptable words; and what was written was upright—words of truth. The words of the wise are like goads, and the words of scholars are like well-driven nails, given by one Shepherd (Ecclesiastes 12:10-11).

HEALINGS AND MIRACLES

The anointing to heal and perform miracles is being augmented in this renewal. While Christians are being renewed and healed emotionally and spiritually with incredible joy by the new wine, they are also being healed physically and receiving the anointing to heal.

All Spirit-filled believers have the authority and ability to heal the sick by faith in God's Word. Yet when there is a special anointing that comes upon you to heal, it is an extra blessing. The gifts of healing in this renewal will often work in operation with other gifts.

I once had a prayer line for the sick at the altar. Many received healing, yet there was a woman who sat back down and did not. Soon after, I received a word of knowledge about a certain sickness that God wanted to heal. It happened to apply to the same woman who had sat down. She came back up for prayer after I gave the word of knowledge and was instantly healed. Why did it happen this way? For one thing, her faith soared when she heard her sickness called out. She knew that only God could have known since she had not told anyone.

The gift of faith works closely with the gifts of healings and miracles. Many times I will shut my eyes for a moment and actually see an image of the sick body becoming whole. Then I will pray according to what I am picturing in the Spirit and not be influenced by what I see in the natural. People seem to receive healing much more quickly this way. It is a matter of faith and the anointing to heal working together. By faith alone you can receive healing, though at times you can face a long battle before it manifests in your physical body. When a special anointing for healing is present to join that faith, it can speed up the healing process.

When people have already heard exciting testimonies about renewal meetings and then travel long distances to attend a meeting, they often arrive full of expectation. Many go with the attitude that if they can just make it there, they are sure they will receive something from God. These people make the trip even if it costs them quite a chunk of money. I believe God honors such faith where people simply trust God to fill them. It is similar to the woman who thought that if she could just touch the edge of Jesus' cloak she would be healed (see Matt. 9:20).

Since we have been renewed and reanointed by the new wine, we have seen the gift of healing multiplied by God's grace. Sometimes He chooses to heal people in a meeting without anyone praying for them. Other times our hands become hot and we know God is telling us to call people up and lay our hands on them. People can be healed by the hundreds, if God chooses, by several words of knowledge that are spoken forth. It is awesome to see people healed when no one has laid a hand on them. In glorious instances such as these people are much more likely to give God all the glory. We serve a mighty and loving God who loves His people so much that He will decide to heal people by His grace at times without any human intervention. To God be the glory!

I believe we are going to see even greater manifestations of healing and miracles upon His menservants and maidservants in our generation. Peter's shadow alone caused people to be healed, as did Paul's handkerchief (see Acts 5:15; 19:11-12). Jesus said that we would do even greater miracles than He did while here on earth (see John 14:12). The most spectacular healing anointings are yet to be demonstrated to the world, not to bring attention to a certain person or ministry, but to bring attention to the Lord Jesus Christ Himself and His salvation message!

Then Philip went down to the city of Samaria and preached Christ to them. And the multitudes with one accord heeded the things spoken by Philip, hearing and seeing the miracles which he did. For unclean spirits, crying with a loud voice, came out of many who were possessed; and many who were paralyzed and lame were healed. And there was great joy in that city (Acts 8:5-8).

Some people will not believe unless they see the supernatural. When Philip went to Samaria, he preached Christ to them, as many ministers do today. Ministers sometimes wonder why nothing seems to happen though their messages are doctrinally correct. This passage says that first of all Philip preached Jesus. Even though he preached Jesus it was not enough for the people. It clearly says that they believed only after hearing and seeing the miracles that he did. To them, it was the sign that what he preached was worth paying attention to as it was backed up by the living God. We are living in a day and age where people think that they have seen and heard it all. For many people, seeing is believing.

Most of the unreached people groups see the supernatural occurring on a regular basis. A nice message with no power confirming it does not interest these people too much. As soon as the message is accompanied with power, they will give their full attention and respect.

The power of God brings attention to the message, which in turn wins the lost. I recently heard a report that approximately 80 percent of Muslims who convert to faith in Jesus Christ do so only after seeing some kind of supernatural manifestation accompany the message of the gospel.

Ask the Lord to use you in this way and believe that He will in the very near future. Step out in faith with His anointing and become the hands and mouthpiece of Jesus.

DELIVERANCE ANOINTING

God is into delivering people from bondages as much as He is into bringing restoration to the Body of Christ. An anointing for deliverance can be acquired in this renewal. This anointing is on a higher level of power than that of healing. As a result of this renewal those who know their authority in Christ will be known by the kingdom of darkness and become a threat to it.

> *The Spirit of the Lord God is upon Me, because the Lord has anointed Me to preach good tidings to the poor; He has sent Me to heal the brokenhearted, to proclaim liberty to the captives, And the opening of the prison to those who are bound...* (Isaiah 61:1).

When demons see the new anointing upon you, they fear. Why? The word *Christ* means "Anointed One." Since the anointing refers to Jesus the Anointed One, demons actually see Jesus instead of you when they see the anointing on your life. They see and fear the "Anointed One." When you are full of the anointing you are full of Jesus. When Jesus approached a person in need of deliverance, the demons would make a big fuss because they knew that His anointing gave Him full authority to cast them out.

When a police officer puts on his or her uniform, he also carries with it an authority to direct traffic. With just one finger he can fearlessly stand in the middle of a traffic jam and direct multitudes of cars and even the biggest trucks. Why? The drivers of the vehicles recognize the authority and the consequences of disobedience that the uniform brings. It is not the officer alone they fear. The officer may be a short and skinny woman, who if she tried to direct traffic without her uniform on, would be in for a rude surprise. It would be foolish and deadly for anyone to attempt that.

The same goes for trying to perform deliverance on people without the anointing of Jesus the Christ, the "Anointed One." If you try it in your own strength you are headed for trouble. Satan will only recognize the authority of the anointing, so put it on *always*. If it is not there then stop in your tracks and seek His face. The seven sons of Sceva learned this lesson the hard way.

> *And the evil spirit answered and said, "Jesus I know, and Paul I know; but who are you?" Then the man in whom the evil spirit was leaped on them, overpowered them, and prevailed against them, so that they fled out of that house naked and wounded* (Acts 19:15-16).

The enemy knew very well who Jesus and Paul were, as they had destroyed much of satan's kingdom. You too will be known when you stand against the evil one with the anointing. Often after Jesus performed great healings, miracles, and deliverances, He would immediately go to a lonely place to be alone with His heavenly Father. When the anointing was on Jesus, He would go where the needs and the people were. When He felt used up and tired, He knew that He needed to get away from the crowd and get refilled at the Source. This is extremely important. We too need to know when the anointing is upon us and when it is waning. Decreasing anointing is a warning to us that we need to get away and renew our spiritual strength.

Are we stronger than Jesus? If He had to get refilled and refreshed before burning out, you can bet that you will too. When you are nearing the point of spiritual and physical exhaustion, you must realize that the Holy Spirit is sounding an alarm to stop and find a quiet place to be alone and renewed by Him. You cannot minister under a heavy anointing such as deliverance for 24 hours a day. That is why some ministers who are very anointed fall. When the anointing is used up they keep trying to minister in their own strength, like the police officer without her uniform trying to direct traffic.

We have experienced some very intense meetings where many deliverances and healings took place. This kind of ministry can take a heavy toll on your body. When we begin to feel the wear and tear of ministry affect us in this way we always try to make time to rest. If you try to do this type of ministry continuously without a break you will not last very long. Deliverance seems to take the most out of people as it requires the exercise of a maximum level of anointing, faith, and spiritual authority.

Jesus knew when power had come out of Him to heal or deliver, as it did with the woman with the issue of blood. Since we have received a renewed anointing, deliverances are taking much less time. A higher level of anointing is in operation as a result of the new wine. This is good news, as this sort of ministry can become less tiring and time consuming. The new wine is simply more of the presence of the Holy Spirit in a more concentrated form. You may already have a strong anointing in a particular area of ministry and so you may not see the need for more. However, you can allow your ministry to be maximized and strengthened if you will allow the Holy Spirit to work even deeper in your life with a new anointing.

Evangelistic Anointing

We have yet to see the most dynamic anointings of evangelism explode all over the world. I believe even the journalists and newspapers will be covering these events daily in the days ahead. Simple men and women will boldly preach the Gospel, accompanied by the miraculous on the streets, in bars, restaurants, prisons, workplaces, and any place where there are lost souls!

This renewal is advancing in several phases. First, God is pruning and restoring the joy of knowing Him back to His Church. Then He is giving out new anointings. And last but certainly not least, He is sounding the alarm for the most powerful evangelistic thrust ever—which will result in the greatest harvest of history as millions upon millions come to receive salvation before the return of our Lord Jesus Christ.

We need to drink in as much of the new wine as we can until we are endued with a spirit of evangelism. This anointing for evangelism is not reserved for "evangelists" alone. Christians who continue to be renewed under this anointing will eventually be overwhelmed with compassion and boldness by the Spirit of God.

Let me share with you an experience that helped me to understand this anointing. I have operated under a specific anointing for evangelism for years, yet it has been renewed. After I was knocked out by the Holy Spirit in the Upper Room in Israel, I led more people to the Lord in the three weeks while I was there than I ever had expected. Evangelism just seemed to flow much more easily as a new boldness came upon me. After receiving more of this anointing in Canada and Florida, the evangelistic anointing became even stronger, and with it came a greater compassion and burden for the lost than ever before. During these moments of being infused with renewed power, I received a word from the Lord that I would see many more souls come into the Kingdom through this anointing. This word sparked an even greater burden for lost souls that at times became like an unquenchable burning fire.

You can get to such a point in this anointing that you feel like you will burst if you don't share Jesus with someone. You become totally oblivious to the fear of people or any other obstacle in your way that would want to hinder you from evangelizing. It is similar to being drunk in the Spirit. You lose your inhibitions about expressing your faith and your passion in life—Jesus! You begin to be filled with an earnestness and an incredible joy at the same time. I believe that the early Church received the fullness of the Holy Spirit which led to masses of people receiving Jesus in a relatively short period of time.

Any Christian can go out and witness out of sheer willpower—and maybe even get some results. But it is much easier when you are witnessing because you are so full of this anointing and compassion for the lost that it becomes a natural overflow in your life wherever you go. This fire and compassion for souls will obliterate the obstacles of fear, intimidation, and self-consciousness that prevent many of us from boldly sharing our faith. Being totally immersed, refreshed, filled with the holy Spirit and renewed, will produce the fruit of much soul-winning if you simply create an outlet for what is in you by sharing it with others. We must eventually reach the harvest if we ever expect this move to explode into even greater power. Don't be satisfied with only some joy and laughter and then stop there, thinking that you have it all. Go much deeper and do not stop receiving new wine until you are filled with an all-consuming burden for the lost that will take you out of your church and out where the lost are waiting for you!

I experimented with the new wine in evangelism as I took a team out on the streets of Paris, which is known for being a difficult city to evangelize. Before we went, I made sure we prayed over the team to impart the new anointing to them as well. As we did, they were laughing in the Spirit and falling to the floor with a fresh, contagious joy. Immediately afterward, we hit the streets. The results were dramatic. We were all filled with such a joy as we could not stop laughing while walking down the street. Those who were normally timid or sluggish became full of boldness brought about by the joy.

When the first man I saw walked past me, I plunged forward to witness to him with great joy and excitement. I laid my hands on the man's legs, which were arthritic, and he was healed! I began to give a word of knowledge to another man about his life. The result was that he gave his life to Jesus and started attending church regularly. Immediately after he received Jesus, I led him into a prayer to receive the fullness of the Holy Spirit. He started laughing with the joy of the Lord—not fully understanding it all but enjoying it. He glowed with a big smile.

We also coordinated our evangelism efforts with an evangelism team from Kensington Temple, a large church in London, which was also experiencing renewal. The results on the streets of Paris were outstanding. God's power was in full swing and again souls were saved and healed right on the street. Because of the renewal we had more access to the gifts of the Spirit in our evangelism and an increase in unity and love. This principle works—whether on the streets or in a large evangelistic meeting with hundreds or thousands in attendance.

Let this new anointing and renewal be channeled into the direction of soul-winning no matter what your gifting or calling is. Just get filled with the refreshing of the Holy Spirit and then go out and be a witness wherever you find yourself! The more you do it the easier it will become. The anointing is to be used, not stored. The more you find ways to give it out, the more you will be able to receive. Paul told Timothy to do the work of an evangelist even though he was a pastor. I remember hearing Nevers Mumba, an African evangelist, say to our Bible school class at Christ For the Nations, "Don't preach like a cool preacher, but preach like a drunk Peter!"

If you are noticing that the anointing is drying up, then go to the Source to get refilled and drunk on the heavenly wine. Then go out and invest it into someone else's life. The slogan "use it or lose it" can be applied to the new wine.

To actually fulfill the Great Commission in our generation will take a mighty missionary fervor of total abandonment to the Holy Spirit's call greater than anything that we have ever seen. It will take men and women so full of the new wine that they will be willing to risk their very lives. Because of their love for Jesus they will carry the Gospel to the darkest hellholes of oppression and suffering in the ends of the earth. This kind of evangelism will be new to many but will resemble the early Church, only with even greater power. Once we have allowed His anointing to consume us, we must start where we are at in our workplaces and with those we meet on a daily basis. In Acts 1:8 the believers were commanded to start where they were in Jerusalem.

After these things I looked, and behold, a great multitude which no one could number, of all nations, tribes, peoples, and tongues, standing before the throne and before the Lamb, clothed with white robes, with palm branches in their hands, and crying out with a loud voice, saying, "Salvation belongs to our God who sits on the throne, and to the Lamb!" (Revelation 7:9-10)

CHAPTER 9

New Wine Draws in New Guests

Then he said to his servants, "The wedding is ready, but those who were invited were not worthy. Therefore go into the highways, and as many as you find, invite to the wedding." So those servants went out into the highways and gathered together all whom they found, both bad and good. And the wedding hall was filled with guests (Matthew 22:8-11).

The wedding party is becoming so grand that the guests are beginning to feel a bit spoiled by all the joy. It is too much to contain only for themselves. "Let us invite those who did not receive an invitation and compel them to come in!" exclaim the guests one to another with the bride and groom in full agreement and anticipation. The guests who go out find it easier to talk to strangers as a new boldness has overtaken them.

As more and more new wine flows into our lives and churches, the wedding party is going to become so enjoyable that even those who were not invited will be envious. Many who were originally invited will not come, as in the parable of the wedding feast in Matthew 22. We must become so full of this new wine in our lives that we are compelled to invite the lost and those in the highways and byways to the wedding feast. Sharing the message of the cross and moving in the power of God with His love and compassion will convince many of these lost souls that the invitation is genuine— and that the new wine has been paid for.

Since our mission is to reach the lost, then what is our message to the world? To the lost we only have one message to preach: we need to return to the message of the cross. The early Church knew the power of this message. The true story of how Jesus Christ was crucified for the world's sins and resurrected in power to bring salvation to the entire human race must be rekindled anew. We need to share the gospel of Jesus Christ in its simplicity. Somehow the Church has tried to intellectualize the Gospel so much that it has in essence diluted its power. We must first start by living the message of the cross before preaching it, if it is to have any effect whatsoever.

For Christ did not send me to baptize, but to preach the gospel, not with wisdom of words, lest the cross of Christ should be made of no effect (1 Corinthians 1:17).

Too many sincere Christians have tried to preach only a one-sided Gospel that says if you accept Jesus all your life's problems will go away and you will live happily ever after. In doing this, Christians believe they are giving a good first impression of Jesus. They think that to also tell people that they are sinners in need of repentance might scare them away. Peter boldly preached the message of the cross to the very people involved in Jesus' crucifixion.

166

Him, being delivered by the determined purpose and foreknowledge of God, you have taken by lawless hands, have crucified, and put to death; whom God hath raised up, having loosed the pains of death, because it was not possible that He should be held by it (Acts 2:23-24).

The result of Peter's sermon about the cross was that 3,000 sinners were saved and baptized in one day. Philip preached Jesus with similar results! Stephen the martyr also preached Jesus and His crucifixion to the very ones who were guilty of handing Jesus over to be killed.

Which of the prophets did your fathers not persecute? And they killed those who foretold the coming of the Just One, of whom you now have become the betrayers and murderers... When they heard these things they were cut to the heart, and they gnashed at him with their teeth (Acts 7:52-54).

Only the message of the cross has the power to truly convert the sinner and give him or her a fair opportunity for salvation. In Stephen's case, it convicted the listeners so much that they killed the messenger instead of accepting the message. In any case the message of the cross will produce results as it rattles satan's cage, thus exposing his defeat. Either revival or persecution will result. If persecution arises, it will ultimately be the seedbed for more revival!

If you study the great revivalists from England and the United States you'll notice that preachers such as Wesley, Finney, and Spurgeon preached the same message. Revival was the result. All people are guilty of the blood of Jesus, not just those who handed Jesus over to be killed. That is why people can be convicted. If caught, a convicted person will either turn himself in or violently oppose you and your message. We, God's people, have strayed from the message of the cross and we then wonder why people are not convicted. You can only be convicted of what you are guilty of. That is how people will get saved and stay saved.

In our society of secular humanism, many Christians have tried to intellectualize the Gospel so as to "meet them where they are at," while excluding the message of the cross, with little or no lasting results. The bottom line is that if the person does not eventually realize that he is a sinner in need of repentance, he cannot and will not truly accept salvation.

Think about it for a moment. What are you telling people to be saved from? After you have witnessed to them, do people feel intellectually better about themselves, or do they feel convicted? You may be wondering how in the world they will understand the simple message of the cross without thinking it to be a foolish fairy tale for children and lunatics. How will such a heavy message tackle the world's logic and human wisdom that would scoff at such foolishness? You may be thinking that this message works well in developing countries, but what about the Western world? Here is what God has to say about dealing with the wisdom of this world:

> For the message of the cross is foolishness to those who are perishing, but to those who are being saved it is the power of God. For it is written: "I will destroy the wisdom of the wise, and bring to nothing the understanding of the prudent." Where is the wise? Where is the scribe? Where is the disputer of this age? Has not God made foolish the wisdom of this world? For since, in the wisdom of God, the world through wisdom did not know God, it pleased God through the foolishness of the message preached to save those who believe (1 Corinthians 1:18-21).

God purposely chooses to use something seemingly foolish to confound those who are thought to be wise in this world. God does not play the world's games of intellectualism with the cross of His

Son, and so we shouldn't either. If we present the Gospel in a worldly way that even slightly dilutes the message, it won't work because the Gospel goes against the world's pattern of thinking. The world wants everything to be logical. If the Gospel was logical the world would only analyze it and go away unimpressed.

The cross is foolishness to the world's way of thinking. Once people have truly heard the message of the cross preached with love through a vessel who is a living testimony of the message, it will mark them for life. It is so powerful a message that it goes against the grain and exposes people's hearts! When preached without compromise it is a message that they will not easily forget. You can't play the world's game; they are too good at it! The cross provides a good shock for a lost soul, and may even short-circuit his human reasoning.

Because the foolishness of God is wiser than men, and the weakness of God is stronger then men (1 Corinthians 1:25).

To God, the message of the cross is a very wise message for victory! Trust God with the results and share the message of the cross to the lost in whatever way He leads you. I am not advocating that you start preaching at the top of your voice concerning the cross every time you see a sinner. Simply make sure that at some point in your sharing that you do not exclude the message of the cross—and most importantly, make sure that you are living it.

PAUL'S LESSON

On his missionary journey to Athens the apostle Paul attempted to intellectualize the Gospel to a certain degree to the philosophical Greeks of his day. It was a brilliant and well thought-out message. Yet it seems to have been the least effective in contrast to Paul's other messages where the power of God was in the frontline of his ministry (see Acts 17). Surprisingly, at this time in Athens there is no record of any baptisms or of a single church being established, and no letter was written to an Athenian church! It was a hard lesson for Paul. Immediately after preaching in Athens, he went to Corinth. There he changed his style of preaching and the delivery of his message. It is quite obvious that his experience in Athens affected him. Take a close look at this verse from his letter to the Corinthians:

And I, brethren, when I came to you, did not come with excellence of speech or of wisdom declaring to you the testimony of God. For I determined not to know anything among you except Jesus Christ and Him crucified. I was with you in weakness, in fear, and in much trembling. And my speech and my preaching were not with persuasive words of human wisdom, but in demonstration of the Spirit and of power, that your faith should not be in the wisdom of men but in the power of God (1 Corinthians 2:1-5).

After his Athens experience Paul came to Corinth in humility with a lack of self-confidence in his human wisdom, though he was highly educated for his day. His message was reduced to Jesus Christ and Him crucified, with the power of God confirming his message. People will only receive what you allow them to put their faith in. If you give them only your persuasive words from your own wisdom, then that is exactly what they will receive—a smart lecture. If you preach the cross to them, then their faith will be in the cross and they will receive the salvation of their souls and the power of God.

JEWS AND GREEKS

The guests who have gone out to bring in strangers to the wedding party are encountering different reactions. Some of these strangers find it hard to believe that the groom would invite them and pay their way to the wedding feast when they are not even friends of the groom or the bride. Others want a sign proving that the invitation was truly given by the groom, if there even is a groom. The new wine and the gifts that the guests have taken along with them demonstrate to these strangers the reality of the wedding party. The true love and concern that the guests have shown for their well-being persuade many to join the party!

> *For Jews request a sign, and Greeks seek after wisdom; but we preach Christ crucified, to the Jews a stumbling block and to the Greeks foolishness* (1 Corinthians 1:22-23).

Jews: Symbolically, in this passage the term *Jews* can refer to those who seek only after signs while totally disregarding the message. It applies to any person who fits into this category of thinking. These kinds of people always want to see miracles, healings, and great demonstrations of power. Even then they still may not be satisfied. Simon the Sorcerer was of such a frame of mind (see Acts 8:9-23). This type of people loves for you to heal them and bless them, but when you mention sin and the cross, they don't swallow it so easily. It is a stumbling block to them. Either they stumble only to receive it, or they will reject it. In either case the message of the cross is the solution.

Even when Jesus was actually on the cross, the religious Pharisees still requested a sign to prove that He was the Messiah. The sign they wanted was for Him to get off the cross! (see Matt. 27:39-42). This same type of people will want you to get off the message of the cross as well! Why? Because it is a stumbling block to them and it convicts them. You can't preach healings and miracles alone to certain people. They need to hear about the cross, and the healings and miracles will confirm your message.

The importance must be on the message, not the manifestations of power. If you give people only healings and miracles, they may even receive one yet go away without the salvation of their souls. Great signs and wonders following the message of the cross will get their attention and allow salvation to be a reality to them that they can put their trust in. Simply put, don't compromise the message of the cross!

Greeks: This type of person is bound by human reasoning, intellectualism, and logic. Much of the Western world follows this thinking pattern. They don't understand the cross—if a message goes against their worldly logic, they tend to label it as foolishness.

Muslims have a similar outlook in several regards. To a Muslim, God (Allah) is all-powerful—a real "man's man," so to speak. From a Muslim's standpoint, it is simply inconceivable for an all-powerful God to come in the form of a lowly baby and actually humble Himself to such a degree for humankind. They believe that it demonstrates great weakness, and Allah is not supposed to be weak. If you continue the story to tell them that Jesus was born on this earth to take away the sins of the world by dying a most humiliating death as a criminal on a cross, it boggles their mind! Their concept of God is totally different from the one we read in the Bible. They cannot comprehend love. God is love! The Muslim asks, "If He is really God, then why does He have to die?" This kind of sacrificial love eludes their thinking. Allah, to most Muslims, is not personal and is not full of such love that he would be willing to die for his people. Allah is a "god" to be feared precisely because he is not merciful.

The message of the cross will shake the whole Muslim concept of God and bring conviction to their souls. If you give a Muslim a logical Gospel other than the cross he (or she) may understand what you are saying—just as he understands 2 + 2 = 4. But will he give his whole life over to Jesus when he most likely will be persecuted and rejected by his family and friends? Probably not. But if you are preaching the cross with signs following, think again! In the last few years, we have seen more and more Muslims receive Jesus, and it has only been because they have been told the full message of the cross accompanied by love, with the supernatural confirming the message.

In present-day Europe—especially France—people have been extremely bound by human reasoning. It has become a "god" to them, much like their greatly respected philosophers of the past. Men like Voltaire spread this demonic thinking across Europe and much of the Western world. This was one of satan's attempts to wipe out Christianity.

By using the foolishness of the Gospel, and more specifically, the cross, the "god" of human reasoning can be obliterated! We are seeing it happen before our very eyes, and it is thrilling! The human philosophy of communism has rapidly been collapsing as believers are growing by leaps and bounds where communism once ruled. As the message of the cross is lived out through His people, I believe that humanism in the West will fall as well.

The same battle is also found within the Church. Those who resist a new move of the Spirit can be influenced by human reasoning. They reason out their own Christianity. People bursting out in joyous laughter during a serious sermon is not logical. Neither is someone shaking violently under the power of God. But God is using some of these things to get their attention and knock out some human reasoning. Religious people do not like it when they are no longer in control. When they do not understand all about something, to them it must not be from God. The Pharisees treated Jesus in a similar manner. We must allow God to use the strategy of foolishness to revive the Church and win the lost!

If church continues as usual, it isn't going to wake up the average Christian and convert the sinner. God loves a good shocker every now and then to wake us up! Jesus did this all the time. Oftentimes while we are ministering, the Holy Spirit will ask us to do something, to which our own mind will respond, "That's crazy, God!" Yet when we obey, incredible things happen. When I have disobeyed because something scared my mind, after it was too late I have known that I failed and lost a chance to demonstrate the wisdom and power of God. We must act opposite to the spirit that is opposing us. If there is a spirit of pride, act in humility. If there is a spirit of hate, use the weapon of love. This is the way of the cross.

> *"For My thoughts are not your thoughts, nor are your ways My ways," says the Lord. "For as the heavens are higher than the earth, so are My ways higher than your ways, and My thoughts than your thoughts"* (Isaiah 55:8-9).

ARE YOU A FOOLISH THING?

We have established the fact that human wisdom, rank, nobility, or power alone cannot influence a soul to accept Christ. But God can easily use simple men and women. In the natural perhaps these simple ones whom God uses could not convince anyone of anything. Yet God in His supernatural wisdom transforms simple people into great ambassadors. In this way God can get all the glory.

> *For you see your calling, brethren, that not many wise according to the flesh, not many mighty, not many noble, are called. But God has chosen the foolish things of the world to put to shame the wise, and God has chosen the weak things of the world to put to shame the things which are mighty; and the base things of the world and the things which are despised God has chosen, and the things which are not, to bring to nothing the things that are, that no flesh should glory in His presence....*

that, as it is written, "He who glories, let him glory in the Lord" (1 Corinthians 1:26-29,31).

Peter astonished the authorities with his great boldness and spiritual authority in Christ, as well as the spiritual wisdom he possessed, though he was only a simple fisherman by trade. Do you feel unpopular, inadequate, and untalented? Do you often wonder how God could ever use you in a great way because you feel foolish sharing Christ in your inadequate state of being? If your answer is yes, then rejoice! You, too, are a candidate for becoming a great ambassador of Christ. God uses foolish things, so it is OK to realize that by yourself you cannot fulfill God's purpose for your life. You are in a good starting place because it is true: you in your own ability and strength cannot accomplish anything for God. Once you have realized this, God can place His ability in you to do things for Him that are far beyond your own natural capabilities. Humility is the foundation and support of this anointing.

It is not that God would not like to use more famous, talented, influential, and rich people for His purposes. The problem is that most people who fall in this category are very aware of it and would have the natural tendency to rely on their own abilities to accomplish His purposes. That would cause a big problem! God would not get all the glory. Somehow humans in their fleshly thinking would believe that really it was them who accomplished great things with their own resources and wisdom instead of God *through* them.

Paul the apostle was an exception. He was greatly talented, skilled, and knowledgeable. He had one of the highest educations and was already influential in his community before accepting Jesus Christ. Paul chose to place all these talents on the altar, choosing not to rely on them. He let them be nailed to the cross. He considered all his learning as "dung" compared to the excellency of a relationship with Christ in which God was in full control (see Phil. 3:8

KJV). When God saw that Paul could be trusted to give Him all the glory, He resurrected his gifts and talents from the cross. He was then all the more used of God with the talents that now were anointed by God. One of the fruits of this was that he wrote most of the New Testament with his newly anointed talent.

At first, Paul tried to use his own influence to further the Kingdom of God. This talent had to be tried first. After Paul's conversion, instead of being very influential, he immediately became very unpopular. The Scriptures imply that the same synagogue where Stephen the martyr preached his last message was where Paul attempted to win the Jews over to Christ. The reaction was that everywhere he went riots arose or people violently opposed him and wanted to kill him. He was not such a popular man anymore (see Acts 21:27-30).

Even the disciples rejected Paul at first because they feared him. They did not accept him so quickly.

And when Saul had come to Jerusalem, he tried to join the disciples; but they were afraid of him, and did not believe that he was a disciple (Acts 9:26).

Despite continued persecution Paul persevered nonetheless in his boldness for Christ. As his ministry was just starting, the believers sent him back to his hometown of Tarsus for approximately 14 years.

I believe Paul must have felt at least slightly humiliated. His influence and all his other "advantages" in life had to first go to the cross. You may have special talents and advantages in this world that you want to use for Jesus. It is an excellent motive, but it will be tried. You may think, *God gave me these talents!* This is true, since every good gift comes from God. But it does not mean that your abilities and talents are anointed yet. You see, once all these dreams and talents have been crucified and newly resurrected, they can be useful and full of His anointing for His purposes.

Let your talents go to the cross. If God chooses to resurrect them, then you know that it was God alone who did so and He will get all the glory. If you try to use your talents and gifts with your own strength without the cross, you will be extremely frustrated—just as Paul must have been when he started out. God always asks us to give Him our best as an offering to Him. He wants those things that are most precious to us.

Isaac was a miraculous gift of God to Abraham and his wife when they were past the age of childbearing. Yet Abraham had to be tested. God said, in essence, "Give Me Isaac!" Abraham obeyed as great distress overtook his soul. *Why would God ask for such a thing?* he most likely pondered to himself. God tested him to make sure that his security, hope, trust, and love were not resting uniquely on Isaac, the gift, instead of God, the Giver of the gift (see Gen. 22).

Most assuredly, I say to you, unless a grain of wheat falls into the ground and dies, it remains alone; but if it dies, it produces much grain. He who loves his life will lose it, and he who hates his life in this world will keep it for eternal life (John 12:24-25).

God is testing our Christianity, our churches, and our ministries in this move of the Holy Spirit. Are our ministries more important to us than our personal relationship with Jesus? God will shake our world until what remains unshaken is left and is His alone. Give your all as a sacrifice to Jesus Christ. If what you give Him is of God, He will resurrect it by His power alone. This is the difference between preaching the cross, as I expounded on earlier, and living the cross.

Why all the sacrifice? Why give up our very best?

That no flesh should glory in His presence. But of Him you are in Christ Jesus, who became for us wisdom from God—and righteousness and sanctification and redemption—that, as it is written, "He who glories, let him glory in the Lord" (1 Corinthians 1:29-31).

The Blood!

The other reason why the message of the cross is so powerful is because it involves blood. The blood of Jesus! When someone gives their all, they give blood. The source of life is in the blood. If you were to lose a leg or an arm you could still survive and live. On the other hand, if you were to lose too much blood, you would die. That is why Jesus' sacrifice was the ultimate sacrifice. Going to the cross meant shedding blood!

In the Old Testament, a person had to sacrifice an animal to cover his or her sins. Jesus became the final sacrifice that did away with the Old Testament ritual of sacrificing an animal to cover sins. Jesus did not do away with the law that there must be a sacrifice. He fulfilled the law by becoming that sacrifice. Jesus' sacrifice was greater because His sacrifice not only covered our sins, He totally erased them as if they had never existed. That's a big difference! It's a much better sacrifice. Since blood is our source of life, the blood of Jesus is our only source of eternal life saving us from our sins. Without this blood, we would die spiritually in our sins, which would lead to total death.

Many religions around the world use blood in their rituals. Satanism is known for sacrificing animals and even human beings. This proves that people know deep down inside that a blood sacrifice is needed to make things right in their lives. They know that something is wrong somewhere in their relationship with the Creator. And so, people will use blood in their rituals because they know it is the most powerful symbol of humankind's source of survival.

What they don't realize is that the price was already paid by the one final blood sacrifice of Jesus. He has done away with the ritual of us providing our own sacrifice for our sins. We don't need to try and provide our own sacrifice, it has already been provided!

Several years ago I was led by the Holy Spirit to take some friends from Bible school and go witnessing on Halloween night. The place was a known hangout for witchcraft and satanism for young adults and teens. Even many of the shops were owned by the satanists. That night, many were wearing their Halloween masks and having a "good time," according to their thinking. We fasted and prayed before we went out, knowing that sin and even demonic sacrifice would take place after midnight. All the worried Christians warned us not to go as it could be dangerous. But we obeyed the Holy Spirit, trusting in God and not in fear.

A young girl walked out of a parked car onto the sidewalk. She looked like a witch. The Holy Spirit revealed to me that it was no costume—she was a witch. The Holy Spirit directed me to speak to her. I told her Jesus loved her, but she just shrugged her shoulders in mockery. Then I spoke a word of knowledge to her that shook her up and also surprised me. I said, "You don't need to do sacrifices anymore. Jesus was the final sacrifice!" At this word she screamed and went into a raging fit as a demonic anger and great fear consumed her. She kept yelling, "That is a lie! Who told you I did that?"

Soon enough she ran away with the full attention of everyone on that street. She had been found out by the living God! God wanted her to know that nothing is hidden from His eyes and that there is a better way. Satan is extremely afraid of the blood! The blood of Jesus caused him to lose the battle for lost souls once and for all on the cross. This blood reminds him of his defeat and soon-coming judgment. When you claim the blood of Jesus, realizing its meaning, you have full protection and great power against satan.

And they overcame him by the blood of the Lamb and by the word of their testimony, and they did not love their lives to the death (Revelation 12:11).

The message of the blood must be preached with the cross. It is the salvation from man's sin. It is the foundational truth for salvation and revival. In this new move of the Spirit, God is restoring to His people the revelation of the blood.

Most people take communion with a sense of religiosity and solemnity. In a sense, many of our communion services are more like funeral services for Jesus' death: we mourn His death and suffering instead of celebrating the victory that His blood represents. Christians often run away from the communion service in fear because of a sin they feel that they don't quite have the victory over yet. They are taught not to partake of the communion if they have any sins in their lives that have not been overcome. This is actually a false teaching that has kept people bound for years! We should be running to the communion table if we have sin that needs overcoming! Why? Because we can say, "Jesus, forgive me for my sins. I repent and take this cup in remembrance of the price that You paid for my sins." Great joy is the result!

We have seen deliverances and outpourings of incredible joy, as well as physical healings, occur during the communion service when the true revelation of the blood is given. Now communion has become an exciting and powerful meeting as Jesus communes with us and we expect His presence.

Communion is like washing our laundry. Normally, if our clothes are dirty, we put them in the washing machine. Christians are fearful that someone will see that they are dealing with sin so they only put their clothes in the washing machine when they think they are clean. That sounds crazy, but that is how most Christians today take communion. Those who feel justified take the communion because they feel like their clothes are clean. Satan has worked to twist the revelation of the blood because he knows that once we really get a hold of it we will walk in great victory and he will walk in greater defeat.

From time to time, my wife and I enjoy taking communion together in our home with this revelation of the blood. We have experienced great visitations with much joy, being renewed in the Lord during these times.

But I say to you, I will not drink of this fruit of the vine from now on until that day when I drink it new with you in My Father's kingdom (Matthew 26:29).

Jesus meant that when He drank this cup again, He would be doing so in victory seated in Heaven with joy. When you take the cup Christ partakes of it with you in a very real sense. He said that He would drink it new. This is the new wine of joy! The word *new* in this passage means "again." When we take communion, Jesus actually partakes of the communion service with us—not in His suffering but in His joy and victory where He is presently seated in Heaven. If you need cleansing, healing, or deliverance, run to the communion table and commune with Him, allowing His blood to transform you and bring victory in your life.

This is the new wine of the Holy Spirit! It is also symbolic of the Great Supper we will have with Him in Heaven. I guarantee you that it will not be a time of mourning and grief. It will be the party of all parties. Go ahead, drink the cup of communion anew. It is the cup of the new wine! You don't even have to wait until the regular communion service at your church. You can have this communion and new wine at home with your family or by yourself any time. With the revelation of the true power of His blood, He truly has saved the best wine for last.

CHAPTER 10

The Fig Tree and the Vine

*...And the tree bears its fruit; the fig tree and the
vine yield their strength* (Joel 2:22).

The new wine is overflowing and the wedding party is full blown with the new guests coming in. Now the bride must be certain that amidst all the joy, she does not forget to honor her parents and allow them to be served the new wine as well. They were the ones who gave her life and without them she would have nothing to celebrate. Before the celebration is over, they must be invited to partake in this joy that they once knew in their own youth.

The parents of the bride are symbolic of Israel and the Jewish people. They, in a sense, birthed us into the Kingdom of God as they were the first to receive salvation and give it away to the rest of the world. The fig tree has always been symbolic for Israel, while the vine refers to the Church. Now, in these crucial times of renewal, we must focus also on the fig tree and not forget Israel. Side by side, we will bear fruit and grow and fulfill our destinies. This subject is ever so crucial if we are serious about accomplishing God's purposes in these days.

I did not originally plan to insert this chapter—knowing that it is still a controversial subject in the Church, as it has been throughout history. I was not certain that people were quite ready for this revelation. Yet God kept pressing upon my heart that the present renewal must be seen in context with God's purposes as a whole, and that now is the proper time to write concerning this subject. Nevertheless, it was a spiritual struggle writing this chapter. I soon discovered that this struggle was because God wanted this to be included in the manuscript, and the forces of darkness certainly did not. I was awakened several nights by the Lord to begin writing this last chapter. I finally did wake up and wrote until about four o'clock in the morning as the pen just seemed to keep writing and the Holy Spirit continued giving me revelation concerning this topic.

We truly need an understanding of the times that we are in prophetically and our responsibility as the Bride. Sooner or later, this subject of Israel and the Church will have to be dealt with. When it is, it will allow the Church to truly fulfill her last days mandate without stopping short. The best way that we can avoid disputes concerning any subject is not to avoid it, but to humbly seek the Lord's wisdom and revelation. Though the subject concerning Israel and the Church may not be accepted by all, we should not let this or any other doctrinal subject separate God's people from one another.

First Chronicles 12:32 states that the men of Issachar had a special gift: they had an understanding of the times to know what Israel ought to do. The Church today needs this gift of revelation like never before. We need to know what God is doing as a whole, and what the Church's responsibility is, in order to gather the greatest harvest ever. Once we have a prophetic understanding of the times we are living in, we will be prepared for what is ahead. There are still prophecies yet to be fulfilled in our generation.

When the Holy Spirit was poured out at Pentecost, Peter preached a sermon that gave an understanding of the times that they were in. In the Book of Acts, he quoted the prophecy of Joel we noted earlier:

> *And it shall come to pass in the last days, says God, that I will pour out my Spirit on all flesh...And it shall come to pass that whoever calls on the name of the Lord shall be saved* (Acts 2:17,21).

Take a close look at Joel 2:32, the verse that Peter quoted. Go ahead and take out your Bible for just a moment and follow with me. Peter did not finish quoting Joel 2:32 but stopped in the middle of the verse with "*...whoever calls on the name of the Lord shall be saved.*" Why did he not quote the whole verse? Have you ever thought about that? The answer is because the latter portion of verse 32 did not apply to that time. That segment of Scripture had not yet been fulfilled. The day of Pentecost was only the beginning of many revivals which have created a spiral effect throughout history climaxing up until our generation. Let us look at what Peter left out in the latter part of Joel 2:32 and see how it now applies directly to our time:

> *...For in Mount Zion and in Jerusalem there shall be deliverance, as the Lord has said, among the remnant whom the Lord calls* (Joel 2:32b).

It literally means what it says: When revival comes and people are being saved and a great harvest of souls breaks out in Jerusalem and Mount Zion (the area where the temple was situated), then Joel's prophecy will be fulfilled!

While we were in Israel we were astonished to see so many Jews receiving salvation. There are literally hundreds and even thousands of Jews in Israel and Russia beginning to accept Jesus as their Messiah on a consistent basis within the past few years! Usually the local messianic churches in Israel see maybe one convert every six months—if they are lucky. Leaders and ministers in Israel say that in 1994 there has been a tremendous breakthrough in the spiritual realm in Israel and Jerusalem. The statistics are turning around. Souls are being saved in Israel at a rate that has not happened since the Book of Acts 2,000 years ago! Something new is happening!

Every time we go to Israel, we are able to lead someone to the Lord. In 2005, we went to a New Age festival in Galilee where over 20,000 Israeli youth converged similar to Woodstock. We were leading them to their Jewish Messiah left and right. Another time, baptizing people in the Jordan in 2005, the Israeli security guard asked what he needed to do to experience the same love and power that he witnessed during the baptisms. He received Jesus (Yeshua) into his heart and we baptized him right there. Other friends of ours, such as Sid Roth, have seen many Russian Jews come to the faith in a single meeting in Israel and the USA! All these testimonies are just in the past three years. In fact, in October 2009, we saw 35 people saved in a single meeting in northern Israel.

The Book of Joel and most of the Bible were not originally divided into chapters and verses when they were written. The very next verse in Joel 3:1 reveals even more:

For behold, in those days and at that time, when I bring back the captives of Judah and Jerusalem…whom they have scattered among the nations… (Joel 3:1-2b).

What exactly does this mean? When Peter preached out of the Book of Joel, the Jews had not yet been scattered from their nation to the ends of the earth. If Peter would have preached the rest of Joel it would not have made any sense or applied to them at that time since they had not yet been fully scattered. That is the reason God had Peter leave all of this revelation out of his sermon until our generation. It was actually meant to be revealed and fulfilled now in our time!

Israel finally became recognized as a nation again in 1948 when Jews, mostly from Europe, immigrated to form a nation of their own. Since then, multitudes of Jews have immigrated to Israel from practically every nation of the world. It has not stopped since. It is happening right before our very eyes. So far, the largest number of Jews to return to Israel in the last few years has been from Russia and its surrounding countries in the northern region of the world. Another interesting note is that the majority of the Jews in Israel who are receiving salvation are those recently coming from Russia and its surrounding nations—and young Israelis in general.

Various motives are causing them to leave the countries that they were in, such as economic hardship, difficult living conditions, and persecution. Some of these are similar to the reasons the Jews left Egypt in the famous Exodus of the Old Testament. Whatever their personal reasons, they are fulfilling what was prophesied long ago. The Scriptures even confirm that what we are seeing now is truly prophetic:

But, "The Lord lives who brought up the children of Israel from the land of the north and from all the lands where He had driven them." For I will bring them back into their land which I gave to their fathers (Jeremiah 16:14-15).

We are yet to see, in the very near future, an ingathering of the remaining Jews from the rest of the world to Israel that is more impressive and greater in number than the great Exodus from Egypt.

Joel 3:1 says, *"in those days and at that time…"* When exactly are *"those days"* and at *"that time"*? They are to occur when:

1. The Holy Spirit is poured out worldwide in His fullness (see Joel 2:28).

2. Fresh prophetic anointings empower God's people in the midst of a worldwide outpouring of the Holy Spirit (see Joel 2:28-29).

3. Signs in the heavens and in the earth occur, referring to natural disasters and calamities upon the earth (see Joel 2:30-31).

4. Worldwide harvest takes place among the Gentile nations (see Joel 2:32a).

5. The Jews begin to return to their homeland from the other nations in greater numbers (see Joel 3:1; Jeremiah 16:15; and many other passages).

6. Jews (including those of political and religious influence in the nation) receive salvation in greater numbers in Jerusalem and the rest of the nation of Israel, and revival breaks out once again as it did after Pentecost (see Joel 2:32b).

Never before in the history of the world have all these conditions in the Scriptures and in the Book of Joel been so near to total fulfillment until now. Could this present renewal be part of the final outpouring that will culminate in the greatest worldwide revival before the return of our Lord Jesus Christ? You decide! Either way, we are in some very strategic times and we must make the most of every opportunity.

And it shall come to pass afterward that I will pour out My Spirit on all flesh... (Joel 2:28).

In Church history, never has revival occurred—to my knowledge—as we have seen since 1994: renewal has been poured out in many different nations, in practically the same month and year, simultaneously producing similar spiritual effects. Historically, God used one nation at a time to usher in revival. Then eventually it would spread to another nation at a slower pace than we are now seeing. God seems to be doing a blitz to speed up the process by pouring the new wine out to many nations at the same time. When asked why there is incredible harvest taking place in his ministry and in his nation in such a short period of time during the height of the revival in Argentina, Hector Giminez, the pastor of the then 150,000-member church in Argentina, said, "God is in a hurry."

As we can clearly see in these passages in Joel and throughout the Bible, the words *Jerusalem* and *Israel* are not only symbolic for the Church but are actually literal in their meaning as well. In these passages these terms were referring to the nation of Israel before the Gentile Church was ever born. Some of these prophecies concerning present-day Israel are still yet to be fulfilled.

For many years, this subject about Israel has been the center of much controversy and confusion. Why? One reason is that Israel did not yet exist as a nation in the world's view until 1948. When major moves of God have occurred in the Church throughout history, the word *Israel* has often been considered to refer to the Church at large. It appeared to the Church that *Israel* must have referred exclusively to the Church because God was moving upon the Church and physical Israel did not yet exist as a nation. It seemed absurd to these Christians to apply the term *Israel* to a nation that did not exist—and seemingly never would.

As the Jews have been blinded to the revelation of Jesus as their Messiah, so the Church has been blinded to the revelation of how physical Israel fits into the whole picture. It is now being revealed. If you go through the Scriptures and take the passages referring to Israel in their dual implications of spiritual and physical Israel, it is amazing how much more revelation you can receive! These verses apply to both today and the near future.

Actually, it is interesting to note that the word *Israel* is mentioned 2,500 times in the Old Testament and 29 times in the New Testament. Never once in any one of these passages is the word *Israel* used to describe the Church. Also, the word *Jew* is mentioned 84 times in the Old and 192 times in the New Testament. The word *Christian* is mentioned only three times in the entire Bible. With this being the case, we would do well to study the Word of God with an open ear concerning the nation of Israel.

Almost every biblical prophecy pertaining to the nation of Israel in the Bible has been fulfilled with the exception of a few more major events and wars still to come (like the wars Gog and Magog and Armageddon, to name a few) as Israel will remain standing but its enemies are destroyed. The remaining prophecies concerning Israel are yet to be fulfilled. I seriously doubt that God will go back on His promises to the nation of Israel, having fulfilled every other one. With this being the case, we can get a better picture of where we're at prophetically. It will help us keep a prophetic eye on news reports and the Word of God concerning Israel and those who worship the God of Israel, the Church!

> *For I do not desire, brethren, that you should be ignorant of this mystery, lest you should be wise in your own opinion, that blindness in part has happened to Israel until the fullness of the Gentiles has come in. And so all Israel will be saved, as it is written...* (Romans 11:25-26).

The *fullness of the Gentiles* coming in refers to worldwide revival and great harvest, some of which is taking place and much more is being prepared. The word *Israel* in this passage cannot be referring to the Church because the passage already makes reference to the fullness of the Gentiles coming in, which is the Church. The Church as we know it primarily consists of Gentiles who receive salvation. And so *Israel* could only mean physical Israel, which is very clear in these Scriptures. This shows a dual aspect to the Great Commission.

> *See! Your house is left to you desolate; for I say to you, you shall see Me no more till you say, "Blessed is He who comes in the name of the Lord!"* (Matthew 23:38-39)

Jesus was emphasizing the fact that Israel would not see their long-awaited Messiah until they would say, *"Blessed is He who comes in the name of the Lord,"* and accept Christ. This is referring to the time when Israel will be revived and receive salvation through Jesus Christ, their Messiah, before He returns again. The dual commission is that all the Gentile nations must hear this Gospel and so must the nation of Israel, which will experience a significant revival after the harvest of the Gentiles is completed. Both the Gentile nations and physical Israel receiving salvation are crucial aspects that need to be accomplished in order to fulfill the Great Commission.

At the time when Jesus said that Israel's temple was left to them desolate in the verse above, their temple was still standing in Jerusalem. It was a prophetic word to Israel that their temple would no longer exist as a means of salvation in the latter days. This was also a word of warning concerning the temple's destruction. Nonetheless, the disciples still marveled at the temple. Jesus then continued to speak prophetically to them trying to make them clearly understand the fate of their temple.

And Jesus said to them, "Do you not see all these things? Assuredly, I say to you, not one stone shall be left here upon another, that shall not be thrown down" (Matthew 24:2).

Israel's temple, which was destroyed several times, is non-existent for the moment. A giant mosque dominates the ancient sight. To the Jews this is a source of great distress because even if they follow their Old Testament rituals to a tee, they still cannot inherit salvation under their own laws. The only way Jews can have their sins covered according to the law is to regularly sacrifice an animal for their sins inside the temple. The temple must be situated on the temple site, which they have no access to at the moment. If they were to sacrifice an animal somewhere else it would not meet the requirements! According to the law, they are damned to destruction, they cannot inherit salvation—and they know it because they have no temple. They are reminded of this as they mourn the loss of the temple at the Wailing Wall, which is the closest location to the original temple site that they are allowed to go for prayer.

There is one solution to Israel's great problem of finding a sacrifice! At this point if they are told that they can accept Jesus as the sacrifice for their sins instead of facing eternal judgment, it brings them hope. This is one great contributing factor as to why there are more and more Israelis receiving salvation. Many Jews have lost hope in their religious rituals as a means of knowing God, though they do respect their ancestors' tradition. God is ripening the nation of Israel in our generation for a great harvest to fulfill Bible prophecy!

I saw this scenario very clearly when I was on the streets of Jerusalem sharing the Good News about the Messiah to the Jewish people. On one occasion, six religious Jewish girls, who were native Israelis, began to weep as the Holy Spirit revealed this truth to them. Their eyes were opened to see that Jesus, their true Messiah, was their only hope and not the temple sacrifices that every religious

Jew awaits in order to save them from their sins. My sister, Melissa, who was on the outreach as well, stood by my side interceding for their salvation. I led them into a sinner's prayer. It was one of the most thrilling conversions I have witnessed! Victory was the result! Only later did another intercessor inform me that another religious Jew was advancing toward me with his fist clenched ready to knock me out. God's protection surrounded me. Thank God for prayer warriors! Only the Holy Spirit could have revealed this truth to the girls by removing the veil in order to give them salvation.

Eventually, the Jews will have their temple as the Scriptures prophesy in the latter days. They will once again sacrifice in their temple, only to see it defiled and desecrated by the "abomination that causes desolation" as prophesied in Revelation and Daniel (see Dan. 11:31; 12:11). After this event many will see that Jesus really is the only possible sacrifice and the nation of Israel will receive salvation in one day. This refers also to the religious and political community who will finally accept this truth and repent.

The times are speeding up. We should not get hung up on when exactly Jesus might return, but we must be prepared at any moment and get to work as we see that day quickly approaching. It is no wonder that local churches in Israel are also experiencing the new wine to prepare them for the harvest. Some of these pastors and leaders made trips to North America and other Western countries where renewal was occurring and brought back this blessing of renewal to their congregations. We who have salvation and a fresh touch of His love and joy in the new wine will make Israel jealous to know their God. This jealousy will play an integral part in the Great Commission as we see in the Book of Romans:

But I say, did Israel not know? First Moses says: "I will provoke you to jealousy by those who are not a nation, I will move you to anger by a foolish nation" (Romans 10:19).

Are we so full of the new wine of the Spirit when we share Christ that we make the world and Israel jealous for what we have? Have you been making anyone jealous lately because of your relationship with the Lord? That is how the world will be saved—when we get full of Him! The sooner we are, the sooner that the world and Israel will be saved. Then we can wrap this chapter of history up and go home to be with our Lord—taking millions with us! We are living in the time of a soon-coming worldwide harvest of souls that most of the patriarchs only wished they could have seen in their day. We are living right smack in the middle of the most exciting times of history!

MAGNIFY YOUR MINISTRY

...And the tree bears its fruit; the fig tree and the vine yield their strength (Joel 2:22).

In the Word of God, the *vine* is referred to as the Body of believers, the Church (see John 15). The fig tree has always been symbolic of the nation of Israel. They are seen here in Joel as bearing fruit together during the great outpouring of the fullness of the Holy Spirit, which we are presently beginning to experience. As the Church is being renewed spiritually, it is being prospered in every way. On the same note, Israel is beginning to prosper because of the Church's spiritual prosperity. The passage in Joel 2 indicates a parallel restoration of the Church and Israel. God's will is that they both prosper and cooperate together in each other's restoration. Israel's survival and ability to accomplish her destiny to ultimately host the return of the Messiah is intrinsically linked to the Church. And the Church must be willing to realize that her destiny to make disciples of all nations before the coming of the Lord cannot be accomplished without Israel's salvation.

When Jesus cursed the fig tree, symbolic of Israel, it was because the tree was not bearing fruit. This was due to the fact that it was the wrong season for bearing fruit (see Mark 11:13-14;20-21). Now the fig tree (present-day Israel) is in its season to bear fruit as the fruit (souls) is ripening for the picking. Souls are riper than ever in Israel and the world, but they will get even riper in the days to come. Joel 2:25-27 speaks of a continued restoration of the nation of Israel. The blessings and benefits that God promises Israel when they are in right standing with God can be applied to any believer who worships the same God of Abraham, Isaac, and Jacob through His son Jesus Christ.

I want us to now look at how you personally can magnify your life and ministry just by applying some simple truths that have been hidden from the Church until recently. Follow with me in your Bible very closely if you would.

*I say then, have they stumbled that they should fall? Certainly not! But through their fall, to provoke them to jealousy, salvation has come to the Gentiles. **Now if their fall is riches for the world, and their failure riches for the Gentiles, how much more their fullness!** (Romans 11:11-12)*

Paul knew the secret to having God's blessing that would enlarge the scope and effectiveness of his ministry. Because Israel rejected the Gospel, we the Gentile Church have been blessed and are prosperous in every way, and have been able to tap into all the rich promises that were originally designated to Israel alone. Are you with me so far? The blessings do not stop there. Paul goes on to explain: if Israel's fall became a blessing for the world, how much more will we be blessed if we partake in Israel's fullness, their spiritual recovery? More specifically, if you partake in evangelizing Israel—either through your prayers and fasting for lost souls and ministries in Israel, by giving financially to support Jewish evangelism, or by actually being a witness to the Jewish people yourself—you will tap into even greater blessings than you ever did before. That is exactly what this verse is saying.

What is curious is that the apostle Paul's mission was primarily to reach the Gentiles. (Peter was specifically called to the Jews.) Yet Paul knew a secret that would enlarge his ability to be blessed in his calling to reach the world: reaching the Jews. The next verse plainly spells it out.

*For I speak to you Gentiles; inasmuch as I am an apostle to the Gentiles, I **magnify** my ministry…* (Romans 11:13).

This is how we can magnify our ministry to the Gentiles as Paul did with God's added blessings!

If by any means I may provoke to jealousy those who are my flesh and save some of them. For if their being cast away is the reconciling of the world, what will their acceptance be but life from the dead? (Romans 11:14-15)

Paul is speaking directly to the Gentile believers in this passage. He affirms his ministry to the Gentiles. Though Paul ministered primarily to the Gentile nations, he always made sure to go and reach the Jews at the local synagogue in whatever country he evangelized. This strategy did not stop the Jews from becoming jealous and furious with him on numerous counts. God magnified and multiplied Paul's efforts greatly in the other nations where God sent him, as well as blessing his writing ministry—to say the least.

Whatever your ministry is and whomever God has placed a specific calling on you to reach, I encourage you to support world missions. But also bless Israel in some way toward salvation, and you will see your ministry and life blessed in a whole new way. By operating this principle in their ministry, countless men and women of

God and their ministries have been greatly blessed, and thus have reached multitudes. Their ministries have reaped and discipled literally hundreds of thousands of souls and blessed the Body of Christ worldwide. The effectiveness of ministries that bless Israel has been magnified as the apostle Paul explains in the Book of Romans. Many of these men and women will admit that this principle greatly contributed to the success and blessings on their ministry.

This principle has a great deal to do with the new wine of the Holy Spirit being poured out today in spiritual renewal. How much more will the new wine be poured out upon us if we are faithful to honor our spiritual parents with salvation? This is one way you can begin to channel out this blessing of renewal to reach the world. God will give you more new wine if He sees that you will use it to bless all people, including Israel.

REMNANTS

As I mentioned, I was very surprised to personally see souls being so open to the Gospel in the land of Israel. And I have been encouraged by the many reports that have come from ministries in Israel. Souls who at first rejected the Gospel are beginning to receive salvation on an ever-increasing scale now in Israel. I have wondered what this could possibly mean in the whole scheme of things. So I began to ask God why this was taking place now in Israel, and how this relates to worldwide evangelism. I always thought that the great harvest of souls and the final revival in Israel would happen later in history—or at least after more nations of the world receive salvation for the first time. If it is beginning to happen now in Israel, how does this affect the Church's role in the rest of the world?

Here is something that I believe the Lord revealed to me:

*God has not cast away His people whom He foreknew. Or do you not know what the Scripture says of Elijah, how he pleads with God against Israel, saying, "Lord, they have killed Your prophets and torn down Your altars, and I alone am left, and they seek my life"? But what does the divine response say to him? "I have reserved for Myself seven thousand men who have not bowed the knee to Baal." Even so then, **at this present time there is a remnant** according to the election of grace* (Romans 11:2-5).

I got my answer. The souls that I saw beginning to receive salvation are not the great harvest quite yet. They are only the first-fruits of the greater harvest to come. These souls were only joining the present remnant of believers. The fact is that the more people who are saved during renewal and the first stages of revival, before the great harvest, the more prepared and numerous we will be to reap the great harvest. In practically every nation of the world there are believers who are the "remnant." At this point the remnant is few in comparison to the nonbelievers.

Many churches at the present time are in a time of renewal, but not quite full-blown revival or the final worldwide harvest, at least in the Western world. Many backsliders are starting to return to the Lord and rejoining that remnant, as well as new converts. These believers are becoming part of the present remnant who will be the ones to reap the rest of the harvest in each nation. God needs more remnant believers saved and anointed to reap the multitudes. That's why just because your city or nation may not be in the revival stage does not mean that you should not go out and win souls by sharing Christ at every opportunity that arises. You should actually create opportunities once you are full of new wine. I'm thankful that someone did not wait until there was a full-scale nationwide revival before they shared Jesus with me. Aren't you equally grateful?

We must not wait around for revival to happen. Go out and get renewed. And then go out and share your faith, adding more believers to the remnant, even if it is only a few. Those few will be in great demand very soon to help you reap *The Big One*. For example, France's evangelical and Protestant Christians are less than 2 percent of the population according to statistics.[1] Imagine if revival were to hit right now and the whole nation was ready to hear the Gospel providing someone would witness to them while they are still open. That 1 percent would have to share the Gospel to the more than 54 million people residing in France in a relatively short span of time. In order to have the greatest effectiveness, that 1 percent—the remnant—must increase. The renewal before the great harvest has already begun in France!

The same principle applies to any city or nation in the world. Go out and witness about Jesus, sharing the message of the cross. Don't wait until the harvest is overwhelming. Jesus knew this problem would arise of having an insufficient number of disciples to do the work.

> *But when He saw the multitudes, He was moved with compassion for them, because they were weary and scattered, like sheep having no shepherd. Then He said to His disciples, "The harvest truly is plentiful, but the laborers are few. Therefore pray the Lord of the harvest to send out laborers into His harvest"* (Matthew 9:36-38).

Jesus had already foreseen this tragedy, as any farmer knows, of finally having a harvest without the manpower to reap it all. In countries that have experienced significant revival and harvest in recent years, like Argentina and China, the number one problem is the lack of Christian leaders (pastors, teachers, evangelists, workers, etc.) to gather and disciple the great harvest.

We need to prepare ourselves for this "problem" and learn from history. Let us go out with this new joy of renewal and use it to gather the rest of the remnant. Look for those who are ripe enough to join the present rank of believers who are helping with the work. Let the anointing of the new wine fill you so full that you will be compelled to be that fearless witness!

SEIZE THE MOMENT

Now that we have an understanding of the times that we are in and how God is preparing such great things for the days that lie ahead of us, we should be left with only one question: "Where do I start in order to be a part of all this?" I firmly believe we must seize this moment in history and make the best of it. Many in past moves of the Spirit have let their opportunity slip through their fingers, only to regret it later. Go and get emptied, renewed, filled, and newly anointed in the new wine. Go yet deeper until God grants you that burning fire and compassion to see the lost saved. Obey whatever the Holy Spirit tells you to do each day. Fulfill that calling, dream, and vision God has placed in your heart.

God is ready to raise up men and women across the globe who are unknown to the world. These masses of believers will soon be in the frontlines carrying the torch of revival around the world. It's not going to be the big name preachers who will carry the revival. It's your turn! You are now entering the faceless nameless revival. Will you enlist in this army? This is an army who will not be concerned as to who gets the glory, but will want only Jesus to receive all the glory and honor. The present renewal will not stop but continue to grow—as will you and your ministry if you allow it. All the saints and angels in Heaven are waiting and watching in anticipation to see who will have the courage to run the last mile of revival and carry the torch to the finish line. Do your generation a favor and "Go for it!" Be desperate for new wine! To our Lord Jesus Christ be all the glory, honor, and praise! So be it.

> *Therefore we also, since we are surrounded by so great a cloud of witnesses, let us lay aside every weight, and the sin which so easily ensnares us, and let us run with endurance the race that is set before us, looking unto Jesus, the Author and Finisher of our faith, who for the joy that was set before Him endured the cross, despising the shame, and has sat down at the right hand of the throne of God (Hebrews 12:1-2).*

ENDNOTE

1. U.S. Department of State, Undersecretary for Democracy and Global Affairs, France, http://www.state.gov/r/pa/ei/bgn/3842.htm.

Partner With Us

Supporting the greater cause of reaching the harvest of souls worldwide connects you to glory and breakthrough greater than what you can accomplish on your own. Together we accomplish many times more. When you give into a ministry that is good ground, that is living in the glory zone and reaching the harvest, God blesses and multiplies what you have given exponentially.

Partners allow us to go beyond and accomplish many times over what we could with our own gifts, strength, or finances. Our ministry travels around the world to reach the lost through crusades, mission trips, revivals, feeding the poor, and a worldwide television program, "The Glory Zone," airing now in every continent. Also, we strongly support Israel through outreaches and by giving generously to ministries that feed the poor. Each year we take hundreds of people to Israel and pray for her revival.

We invite you to be part of our family and enter into the shared blessings of partnering with us to take the Gospel to all people.

Presently our television program is bringing in many souls and opening doors to hold evangelistic campaigns in many hard-to-enter countries. As you give and pray, we believe that you will receive a portion of the same favor, glory, and mantle that has been placed on this ministry. If you feel this ministry is good glory ground in which to sow, please consider becoming a partner with a monthly donation or a larger one-time gift to spread the Gospel to the ends of the earth.

To become a partner, visit us online at: www.thegloryzone.org.

Contact Us

To contact David Herzog Ministries for crusades, conferences, or revival meetings, or to receive more information about this ministry, please use one of the following ways.

E-mail us at: office@thegloryzone.org

Visit our Website at: www.thegloryzone.org

Write us at:

David Herzog Ministries
P.O. Box 2070
Sedona, AZ 86339
U.S.A.

For those interested in receiving our prayer/partner letter, please include your name and address.

Additional copies of this book and other
book titles from DESTINY IMAGE are
available at your local bookstore.

Call toll-free: 1-800-722-6774.

Send a request for a catalog to:

Destiny Image₀ Publishers, Inc.

P.O. Box 310
Shippensburg, PA 17257-0310

*"Speaking to the Purposes of God for This
Generation and for the Generations to Come."*

**For a complete list of our titles,
visit us at www.destinyimage.com.**